ACOUSTIC GUITAR GUIDES

PERFORMING ACOUSTIC MUSIC

STRING LETTER PUBLISHING

Publisher: David A. Lusterman
Editor: Jeffrey Pepper Rodgers
Designer: Gary Cribb
Production Coordinator: Christi Payne
Marketing Manager: Jen Fujimoto
Production Director: Ellen Richman

Cover photographs: top right, Jay Blakesberg; top left, Anne Hamersky; bottom center, Tony Harrison.
Interior photographs and illustrations: Cecilia Van Hollen, pp. 11, 66 (top); Janet Smith, p. 13; Tony Harrison, pp. 19, 21; Stewart O'Shields, p. 25; Paul Kotapish, pp. 28, 40, 42, 51, 77, 85; Bonnie Marvel, p. 30; Andrew Madoney, p. 37; Judith Antonelli, p. 39; Kevin J. McCormick, p. 45; Collin Golbie, p. 46; Jennifer Berman, p. 52; Anne Hamersky, pp. 54, 90; Gary Cribb, p. 58; Scott Blum, p. 63; Paul Natkin, p. 79; Mackie Designs, p. 83.

David A. Lusterman, Publisher
ISBN 1-890490-22-9

Printed in the United States of America.
 This book was produced by String Letter Publishing, Inc.
PO Box 767, San Anselmo, California 94979-0767
(415) 485-6946; www.acousticguitar.com

Library of Congress Cataloging-in-Publication Data

Performing acoustic music.
p. cm.-- (Acoustic guitar guides)
ISBN 1-890490-22-9
1. Rock music--Vocational guidance. 2. Guitar--Methods (Rock) I. Series.

ML3795 .P415 2000
781.4'3'--dc21

00-0423689

STRING LETTER PUBLISHING

contents

5 **Introduction**

6 **About the Authors**

10 **A Letter from Backstage** JEFFREY PEPPER RODGERS

GETTING READY

13 **Taking the Stage** DALE MILLER

15 *Suzanne Vega's First Gig*

16 *Guitar Careers*

19 **Performing Tips and Tactics** KRISTINA OLSEN

22 *Leo Kottke on Stage Rap*

25 **Memorizing and Mental Preparation** SHARON ISBIN

26 *Remembering the Words*

27 *Making Faces*

28 **Making Stage Fright Work for You** JOHN HERNDON

30 **Troubleshooting Your Show** MIKE BARRIS

31 *Fingernail First Aid*

33 **How to Find People to Play with** SUSAN STREITWIESER

35 *Setting Up an Open Mic*

36 *Resources for Finding Musicians*

FIRST GIGS

37 **Busking** JUDITH ANTONELLI

40 **Bookstore Gigs** TEJA GERKEN

42 **How to Succeed as an Opening Act** COSY SHERIDAN

45 **Playing in Restaurants** GARY JOYNER

51 **House Concerts** COSY SHERIDAN

54 **Being a Side Musician** SCOTT NYGAARD

58 **Getting Paid** DAVID HAMBURGER

CHOOSING GEAR

60 **Sound Decisions** HARVEY REID

63 **Amplifying Your Guitar** CHRIS PROCTOR

65 *Starter Questions*

67 *To Install or Not to Install a Pickup*

70 *Using Effects*

71 *Signal Loss*

75 *Soundhole Covers*

76 *Pop-Free Cables*

77 **Bringing Your Own Microphones** MARK FRINK

79 *All around the Mic*

80 *Jody Stecher on Mic Techniques*

SOUND CHECK

82 **PA System Basics** MARK FRINK

84 *Room Acoustics and Feedback*

85 **Creating a Sound-Check Routine** MARK FRINK

86 *Advice from Top Soundmen*

89 *Notching Out Feedback*

90 **Getting the Best Guitar Sound on Stage** SCOTT NYGAARD

91 *What's the Buzz*

92 *David Tanenbaum on Miking a Classical Guitar*

93 *Ground Hum*

94 **How to Get Good Sound at the Last Minute** RICK TURNER

REFERENCE

97 **A Complete Glossary of Amplification Lingo** RICK TURNER

introduction

So you've been playing for a while now—picking quietly in the living room, maybe singing a little, working up a small repertoire of songs or instrumentals that sound pretty good. You've mustered the courage to pull out your instrument in front of family or friends—maybe even joined an informal jam or two. But now you're ready to take the next step, to share your music with a larger group of people in a public space, whether it be a café, club, church, or street corner. It's an exciting transition but an intimidating one, too, and it can be very hard to ferret out advice that's reliable and applies to your situation and aspirations.

Performing Acoustic Music was created just to fill that gap: to offer acoustic musicians a comprehensive source of information, inspiration, and real-world advice written by performers who've been in exactly your position. Even if you've got some gigs under your belt, you've always got questions about how to improve your stage craft, your repertoire, and your gear, and this book will help you find the answers.

Here's how the book is organized. In the opening section, you'll find all sorts of useful tips and techniques (most learned by the authors the hard way) on getting ready to perform. The next part spotlights the kinds of diverse venues that offer great opportunities for your first (or umpteenth) gigs—bookstores, restaurants, house concerts, subway platforms, etc. So much of the acoustic music scene operates outside of the club circuit that a little creative thinking about gigs will carry you a long way.

The balance of these pages is devoted to live sound, because a hard truth of being an acoustic musician is that translating your living-room sound into the plugged-in world of PA systems requires much more knowledge and experimentation than it does for electric players. ("It's ironic," Rod Cook, guitarist for the Laura Love band, once said to me. "My acoustic setup is way more electronic than my electric setup is—way more wires and cords being used.") To help you on this sonic quest, we've pulled together amplification advice from the experts—both players and sound engineers—starting with how to choose the right gear and proceeding right through how to do a successful sound check.

Have a great gig.

Jeffrey Pepper Rodgers
Editor

ACOUSTIC GUITAR

about the authors

JUDITH ANTONELLI

Judith Antonelli is a freelance writer and editor living in Boston, Massachusetts. She has played the acoustic guitar for 35 years, beginning with The Joan Baez Songbook when she was 12 years old. She loves to sing and counts among her vocal role models Stevie Nicks, Grace Slick, Chrissie Hynde, and Natalie Merchant. She has recently begun a songwriting partnership with friend and fellow musician Leonard Eisenberg and is also learning to play the mandolin.

MIKE BARRIS

Toronto native Mike Barris is a swing and blues guitarist, singer, and guitar teacher based outside of New York City. He has been performing at festivals, coffeehouses, and clubs since the late '80s and has presented workshops on performance at festivals, libraries, and schools. Barris writes for such publications as *Down Beat* and *Jazz Journal International* and has released a CD, *Delta Sunrise* (Adirondack), with his acoustic swing band Delta Sunrise.

MARK FRINK

Mark Frink lives in Portland, Oregon, where he acts as *Mix* magazine's sound reinforcement editor and works as a sound engineer. He has mixed sound for the Metropolitan Opera, Tony Bennett's unplugged tour, k.d. lang, Pavarotti, the Super Bowl, and Meredith Brooks, just to name a few. Frink earned his degree in economics from the University of Massachusetts at Amherst in 1981 and spent the next decade with Sun Sound Audio, touring with Crystal Gayle, Marshall Crenshaw, Suzanne Vega, Eric Clapton, and 10,000 Maniacs. He also established the Wintertide Coffeehouse in Martha's Vineyard. He can be contacted at www.markfrink.com.

TEJA GERKEN

Before he became *Acoustic Guitar* magazine's gear editor, fingerstyle guitarist Teja Gerken managed a music store, apprenticed with a guitar maker in Paracho, Mexico, and worked as a freelance translator and desktop publisher. When he is not busy reviewing music equipment, Gerken hosts a fingerstyle concert series at an Emeryville, California, venue called Strings, where he has shared the stage with many of today's top pickers. His Web site, www.tejagerken.com, features articles on a variety of guitar-related subjects as well as samples of his debut CD *On My Way* (LifeRhythm Music).

DAVID HAMBURGER

David Hamburger is a guitarist, teacher, and writer who lives in Brooklyn, New York. He has toured with Salamander Crossing and Five Chinese Brothers and appeared on recent recordings by Chuck Brodsky and the Kennedys. A regular instructor at the National Guitar Summer Workshop, Hamburger has written three instruction books, including

The Dobro Workbook. His latest solo recording is *Indigo Rose,* on Chester Records (www.songs.com).

JOHN HERNDON

John Herndon is a poet, journalist, musician, and teacher who lives in Austin, Texas. In the last 25 years, he has recited his poetry all over Texas as well as in Seattle, San Francisco, Santa Fe, New Orleans, New Jersey, China, and Mexico. He currently performs solo and with his brother in an acoustic-electric band called Half Moon. Herndon has written a number of books, including *Survival Notes* (Latitudes), *Poems from Undertown* (Eco-Tropic), *Where Three Roads Meet* (Cedarshouse), and *Proof That the World Is Real* (Tantrum).

SHARON ISBIN

Winner of the Toronto, Munich, and Madrid competitions and *Guitar Player* magazine's Best Classical Guitarist award, Sharon Isbin has given sold-out performances in New York's Carnegie Hall, Amsterdam's Concertgebouw, and London's Wigmore Hall, among many others. She has made over 20 recordings, including *Journey to the Amazon* (Teldec Classics), which received a 1999 Grammy Award nomination. Isbin directs the guitar department at the Juilliard School, has premiered nine new concertos for guitar and orchestra, and authored the *Classical Guitar Answer Book* (String Letter Publishing) and the first performance editions of the Bach Lute Suites in collaboration with Rosalyn Tureck. For more information, visit www.sharonisbin.com.

GARY JOYNER

St. Paul, Minnesota, resident Gary Joyner sings and plays acoustic guitar in restaurants, clubs, coffeehouses, and on concert stages and cruise ships. He teaches fingerstyle guitar, guitar tunings, songwriting, music theory, performance, creativity, and harmonica. Joyner cites Bob Dylan and Leonard Cohen as songwriting influences and credits Captain Beefheart, Harry Partch, Miles Davis, Joe Zawinul, and Herbie Mann for teaching him how to listen. His nonmusical influences include writers Henry Miller and Jack Kerouac, as well as painters Paul Klee and Pablo Picasso.

PAUL KOTAPISH

Paul Kotapish, *Acoustic Guitar*'s assistant editor, joined his first band, the Savages, at the age of 12 and has been playing music ever since. He has toured extensively and recorded numerous albums with Irish fiddler Kevin Burke, the Hillbillies from Mars (www.hillbilliesfrommars.com), and others. Kotapish recently completed work on a CD that meshes Grateful Dead originals with traditional Irish music. "It's better than it sounds," he insists. In addition to writing and performing, he enjoys teaching mandolin and guitar at the Puget Sound Guitar Workshop, Pinewoods, and the California Coast Music Camp.

DALE MILLER

Dale Miller is a fingerstyle guitarist, guitar teacher, music store owner, freelance writer, and computer consultant living in Berkeley, California. He has two book/CD combos available from Mel Bay Publications, and his 1974 LP *Fingerpicking Rags and Other Delights* has been rereleased by Fantasy Records. He has contributed to a number of String Letter Publishing books, including *Fingerstyle Guitar Essentials* and *Acoustic Blues*

Guitar Essentials. In addition, Miller has recorded a self-produced CD of fingerstyle and slide guitar duets titled *Both of Me,* which is available through his Web site at www.dalemiller.com.

SCOTT NYGAARD

Scott Nygaard, *Acoustic Guitar* magazine's associate editor, is an accomplished guitarist with more than 25 years' experience. He has performed and recorded with such artists as Laurie Lewis and Grant Street, Tim O'Brien and the O'Boys, David Grisman, and Jerry Douglas; released two solo albums, *No Hurry* and *Dreamer's Waltz* (Rounder); and been nominated for a number of Grammies for his work on other artists' CDs. He lives in San Francisco and performs with the Quirks and singer Chris Webster. His instructional video, *Bluegrass Lead Guitar,* will soon be released by Stefan Grossman's Guitar Workshop.

KRISTINA OLSEN

Multi-instrumentalist and singer-songwriter Kristina Olsen spends ten months a year touring around the world playing music and gathering inspiration for her writing. Olsen was born in San Francisco and grew up in Haight-Ashbury during the '60s, and she now calls Venice, California, home. She has released eight recordings, including *The Truth of a Woman* (Take a Break), which was ranked No. 1 of surveyed folk airplay for October '99. One of the highlights of Olsen's year is teaching slide guitar at summer music camps.

CHRIS PROCTOR

Chris Proctor is a nationally renowned performer and composer for the steel-string guitar. A former U.S. National Fingerstyle Guitar Champion, he has toured internationally and released six recordings of his original compositions and arrangements and four books of his transcriptions. He teaches at hundreds of guitar workshops and clinics nationwide and has also recorded an instructional video for Homespun Tapes. Proctor is currently working on a CD to be released in the summer of 2000, and a recently recorded piece will be included in a Windham Hill sampler scheduled for spring release. For details, visit www.chrisproctor.com.

HARVEY REID

Songwriter and multi-instrumentalist Harvey Reid has honed his craft over the last 30 years in countless clubs, festivals, street corners, cafés, schools, and concert halls across the nation. He has absorbed a vast repertoire of American music and woven it into his own colorful and distinctive style. Reid won the 1981 National Fingerpicking Guitar Competition and the 1982 International Autoharp competition. His 13 solo albums on Woodpecker Records (www.woodpecker.com) showcase his mastery of many instruments and styles of acoustic music, from folk and country to slide and blues.

JEFFREY PEPPER RODGERS

Jeffrey Pepper Rodgers is the founding editor of *Acoustic Guitar* magazine and has been writing extensively on the acoustic music scene since 1989. His profile of Joni Mitchell's guitar and lyrical craft appears in the book *The Joni Mitchell Companion* (Schirmer), and his interview with Dave Matthews and Tim Reynolds is included in their *Live at Luther*

College songbook (Cherry Lane). Rodgers plays acoustic guitar and tabla (the north Indian drum) and has performed as a duo with his brother Andy and with the acoustic rock quartet Heavy Wood. He has been putting words and music together since he was a teenager, and his all-acoustic, all-original homegrown CD, *Traveling Songs,* can be sampled at www.jeffreypepperrodgers.com.

COSY SHERIDAN

Cosy Sheridan is winner of both the Kerrville Folk Festival's New Folk award and the Telluride Bluegrass Festival's Troubadour award. She has been a professional touring musician for the past 15 years, and her songs have carried her to such varied venues as Carnegie Hall and the *Dr. Demento Show*. Sheridan studied voice at the Berklee School of Music and guitar with Guy Van Duser and Eric Schoenberg. She has released five albums on the Windriver/Folk Era and Waterbug labels, including her latest, *Grand Design.*

SUSAN STREITWIESER

Susan Streitwieser has been performing for 20 years. She started out in college with the usual coffeehouse guitar/vocal solo gigs and soon graduated to clubs and festivals with her a cappella quintet the Distractions. In 1991 she formed her folk-pop band Susan's Room, which has gigged throughout the U.S. and released four albums, including the mostly acoustic *Thinner* (1999). Streitwieser has also written and recorded *The No Scales, Just Songs Vocal Workout,* a song-based method for strengthening the voice. For more information, visit www.songwriter.com/susan.

RICK TURNER

Rick Turner has been designing, building, and repairing acoustic and electric guitars for 35 years. He got his start in the music business as an RCA recording artist with the band Autosalvage, played guitar with Canadian folk duo Ian and Sylvia, and also worked for years as a live sound engineer. He designed magnetic pickups and cofounded Highlander Musical Audio Products before beginning his current company, the Renaissance Guitar Corp. Turner is also a regular contributor to *Acoustic Guitar* magazine and has been a contributing editor since 1991.

BOB WOLSTEIN

Bob Wolstein has worked with recording and sound reinforcement technology since the 1970s. Between 1979 and 1984 he toured as a chief technician for Earth, Wind, and Fire, James Taylor, Linda Rondstadt, Weather Report, and Men at Work. He has also redesigned and rebuilt many professional recording studios, including Tacoma Recording Studios in Santa Monica, California, where he engineered sessions with artists including Taj Mahal, John Renbourn, and Tal Farlow. In 1991, Wolstein cofounded Highlander Musical Audio Products, which manufactures professional amplification equipment for acoustic musicians. The company supplies pickups and preamps to National Reso-Phonic as well as a custom-designed preamp for the Renaissance Guitar Company.

A Letter from Backstage

Jeffrey Pepper Rodgers

Dear Musicians,

Taj Mahal, Jorma Kaukonen, Peter Rowan, John Lee Hooker—these and many other familiar faces peer down on us from every wall. "Live at the Sweetwater," the posters say. I can picture the room upstairs packed with bodies, sweating and swaying to the music; the line of eager ticket buyers extending down the street; the bouncer collecting crisp bills; the tap filling empty glass after empty glass. What could *we* possibly be doing here, in this same basement where Ry Cooder has tuned up his guitar? That image both inspires and intimidates me as I sit here, tweaking my B string, listening hopefully for signs of intelligent life upstairs.

It's a Tuesday night in early winter, and my band, Heavy Wood, is getting ready to play some music in this venerable club. A few hours ago, Andy, Jay, Steve, and I were leaving our respective day jobs and joining the flow of rush-hour commuters. Now we've unloaded our gear—acoustic guitars, upright bass, and percussion—and done the sound check. I've changed into my black boots and favorite guitar-playing shirt, and I'm trying hard to shed my after-work lethargy and summon the energy that will make our songs come alive. It's always a tough transition, like unscrewing one head and attaching another.

Heavy Wood is not what you'd call a workhorse club band. We've played at a few venues around the Bay Area, but we spend most of our time together working on new songs, polishing arrangements, and recording the tunes that come out the best. A few years ago, we lucked into getting heard by the owner of this club, which has a much larger reputation than seating capacity, and we played a split bill with another local acoustic band. Between the four band members, we rounded up enough relatives, friends, and fans to come hear us that we've been invited back, several times now. It's our best gig by far, which both energizes me and makes me worry like crazy about what's going on upstairs. How many tables are full? Is Denise, the waitress, looking at her watch and preparing herself for a long, dull night, or is she pleasantly surprised by the figures filing in from the street?

I can't suppress a yawn—it's one of my expressions of nervousness. The other is the faint gnawing in my stomach, which usually begins by four o'clock in the afternoon and discourages me from having any sort of real dinner before a gig. It helps to have something to occupy this empty time between sound check and the first set: I still have to write out the set list to take on stage. After I jot down a song title, I listen in my mind to the final chords and imagine how the next song's opening riff will sound a few moments later. When I'm finished, I attach my list with electrical tape to the dark upper bout of my guitar. Although we have set aside one song for a possible encore, it's not our best song and we don't really expect to play it: this is, after all, Tuesday night, and we are not like the seasoned players who look down on us from the walls, clutching their guitars with the ease and assurance that come from many years of albums, stages, and encores.

We're not alone in this position, perched between amateur and professional music making. In fact, we comprise a high percentage of the musicians who climb onto stages and stools every night. Our ranks include those who have dreamed of making a living as a musician but settled for a secure day job instead and perform occasionally to keep the flame alive, those who tried to make a living as a musician but got discouraged and went to Plan B, and those who never wanted to make a living as a musician but still get out there because they crave the buzz of live performance. We're the wannabes, the not-ready-for-prime-time players, loiterers on the fringe of the music business. We're not quite pros—we don't have managers, tour buses, press clips, our band names stenciled on the amps—but we're no less serious and passionate about what we do. Our demo tapes clog the mailboxes of people in "the business," and our hands and vocal cords fill clubs, restaurants, and coffeehouses around the world with music.

Jeffrey Pepper Rodgers on guitar.

Considering how many musicians like me are out there both comforts me and makes me feel vaguely anxious. From the amateur point of view, a fellow musician is an ally, a kindred spirit, a jam partner; from the professional angle, that same musician is another person nagging the same record companies and club owners—maybe sending a slicker demo and glossier photo and getting the gig rather than you. Even for those of us whose typical income from a gig is approximately enough to cover a burrito and a set of strings, this competitive aspect is insidious. It's not the money that matters, it's the pride. It's the judgment of your music implied in every unreturned phone call and rejected tape, the preference expressed for someone else's creations. When you're searching for gigs or that Holy Grail of the record deal, for every success there might be 50 rejections, and each one stings. What does that slimy booking guy with the tattoos know about good music anyway?

In my case, it's the songs I write that keep me going at this racket, year after year. If I don't play these songs of mine, who will? Although there's an enduring satisfaction in the act of crafting a melody, honing the words, and finding the right instrumentation, eventually the best songs beg to be heard by an audience beyond your spouse, your dog, and a few friends at a party. Until I've put those certain songs out there for an audience, it's as if they aren't quite finished. Even if the chance to perform comes only once in a while and under less-than-ideal conditions, I need to feel those songs emerge from my chest and guitar and go in search of sympathetic ears. And there's nothing more gratifying than a sign that a song has connected with someone—an appreciative nod glimpsed in the back row, a more-than-polite round of applause, a genuine compliment between sets.

Of course, these high-minded intentions don't mean a lot when the guy back by the pool table wants to hear "Sweet Melissa" and reminisce about his high school girlfriend, rather than puzzle over some weird tune he's never heard before and will probably never hear again. Playing original songs for people who don't own your CD is an uphill battle and can definitely limit your gig opportunities. Playing a repertoire of sometimes folky, sometimes jazzy, sometimes rocking tunes with a band, rather than the tinkly background music people expect from acoustic musicians, adds another barrier to the success of Heavy Wood, Inc. Not loud enough to compete with electric blues bands but too loud for the pensive poets at the Cafe Milano, we often wind up stuck, as it were, between rock and a soft place.

But this is no time to grouse about the frustrations of finding good gigs. Here we are, about to take a stage where some esteemed musicians have held court. This is our night—that's our name by the door. Steve plucks a harmonic on his bass, eyeing the digital tuner. I run my fingers up and down the fretboard to limber them up, while Jay tells Andy about the show by the Band that he caught a while back.

"Five minutes," Sue calls out from the stairwell. "Alright?"

"Alright," I say. We were hoping she'd be here tonight. Almost every time we've played here, Sue has been running the mixing board, and she's gotten better and better at putting across our quirky ensemble sound. She knows that Andy strums and sings much louder than I do, that I use my guitar mic for percussion on a few tunes, that the congas and cowbell need to be boosted in the mix. We're spoiled, having a house sound person who's familiar with our music. At just about every other venue where we're not using our own PA, a sound check—if we get one at all—consists of someone plugging in cords, hitting the power switch on the board, and, if each instrument and microphone emits a noise of some sort, heading for the bar. One of the cruel ironies of being an acoustic musician is how your beautiful and subtle playing, chiseled to perfection over many years, usually sounds like the harpsichord patch on a $50 Casio keyboard by the time it comes out of the speakers, while the Neanderthal rockers who come on afterward sound like they're on tour promoting their latest platinum CD.

"OK, guys," Sue says. We grab our instruments; I take a deep breath. At the top of the stairs, I spot a respectable number of bodies at the front tables—even a few faces I don't recognize. It's not a huge crowd, but not bad at all for a Tuesday night, and definitely enough to justify the phone calls, the postcard mailing, the purchase of that new guitar cord. As we plug in and settle into our places, Sue turns up the stage lights and speaks into her microphone back at the board.

"Ladies and gentlemen," she says, "welcome to the Sweetwater. Tonight we have a special show by four guys who I've known since they were just little kids." She's lying. Andy and I laugh; the crowd is now turned toward the stage, sipping drinks, giving us a once-over. Sue wraps up her introduction, "Please welcome Heavy Wood."

There's a small wave of applause. Andy strums an F♯—the opening chord of "Come On Home." I count out four, and we nail the downbeat. The groove is solid—the interlocking strums, the bass octaves, and the snare rim shots sound good and set my head bobbing with the beat. Once the music begins, my nervousness vanishes, as it always does. Day job? What day job? I close my eyes and the song carries me away, inviting the audience to come along for the ride.

Taking the Stage

Dale Miller

For many musicians, the move from playing alone to performing for an audience is a large and intimidating step. When you play alone in your room, you only have to live up to your own expectations and criticisms (which can be hard enough), while an outside audience—whether it be friends, family, or strangers—introduces a whole range of variables and fears. But the rewards of sharing music with others more than justify the difficulties.

Still, playing for others is tough. You need the courage to overcome your fear and the commitment to keep at it. It can be done, though, and I'd like to share a few tricks to help you get there. I've learned these lessons over the years, usually the hard way.

GEARING UP

Rehearse well. Play your tunes exactly as you will on stage. Don't stop in the middle and start over. Quite a few players develop the habit of never playing a song all the way through. You shouldn't be in a situation where the first time you perform a piece from beginning to end is on stage.

Keep in mind that you don't really know a song until you know it. That sounds facetious, but I'm serious. You don't really know a piece until you can play it with cold hands to a rude audience through a lousy PA system. Practicing at home with a couple of restarts just doesn't cut it. There's no disgrace in not knowing a piece. Everyone goes through the same learning curve. If you make mistakes it doesn't mean you have no talent; it means you don't know the piece yet. It's that simple. Just keep practicing.

Make your rehearsal as realistic as possible. If you're going to play standing, practice standing. If you'll be using a mic, practice in front of a mic even if it isn't plugged in.

Warm up. I've always felt that the best way to warm up is to play stuff you aren't planning to play on stage. If you're nervous to begin with, it's easy to second-guess yourself as you warm up ("Am I really playing this right?"). You should know the tunes you're planning to perform so well you don't need a last-minute review. If you're at an open mic, jamming with some of the other musicians is a good way to loosen up, although you should be aware of the occasional bit of gamesmanship like, "Gee, you're using a bad fingering there," or "You look kind of sick," or "I really prefer Joe Blow's version of that song."

A lot of folks do exercises to warm up, and one guitarist I toured with, the late Marcel Dadi, warmed up by vigorously shaking his hands for three or four minutes. It's impor-

Dale Miller on wood and steel.

tant to warm up your voice as well. But you can overdo it. Don't leave your best performance in the dressing room, and don't start a 45-minute set with your most difficult tune.

Respect the music. Develop the philosophy of being a servant to the music. See yourself as the humble gateway through which the music passes to be shared and enjoyed. Sure, you may be full of insecurities and perceived weaknesses (I know I am), but the music is great and deserves to be heard.

Visualize success. Don't let your ego go completely, though. Have the courage to see yourself as a success. Someone has to be a star. Develop the attitude, "Of course they're going to like me."

Keep things in perspective. Even if you totally screw up and are booed off the stage, the world will keep revolving and the people who booed will pass you in the street a week later and won't remember a thing. Actually, getting booed off the stage is extremely unlikely. Being ignored is usually as bad as it gets. It's important to realize that being paranoid is being self-centered. Thinking, "They're all laughing at me and hate me" implies that "they're all thinking about me." People don't really care that much. They've got their own problems. Try to maintain a sense of humor about it all.

Set a reasonable goal. You can minimize your chances of failure if you don't make your first public venture an audition or open mic at one of the top clubs in town. It's best to start by playing for your friends and family. When the mood is really mellow and relaxed, pull out your guitar and say, "Want to hear a tune I've been working on?" and try it out. But treat them as an audience. Play the tune all the way through as if it were a professional performance. Don't stop if you make a mistake and don't apologize. Develop the habit of always being "on stage" whenever someone is listening to you.

I feel that some musicians actually seek out failure as an excuse to back off from playing on stage. They'll set an unreasonable goal, fail, and retreat into self-pity. Avoid this temptation and stack the deck in your favor.

Use your fear. You're sure to be nervous whatever you do, so learn how to use that energy. It will get easier. It's hard to believe it when you're first starting, but complacency can become your enemy after you've been performing for a number of years. In fact, many experienced entertainers welcome some apprehension because it creates energy. One warning, though: when you're pumped up, if you're not careful, you're going to play everything about twice as fast as you rehearsed it.

Beware of drugs. Quite a few musicians have been ruined by drugs, especially alcohol, heroin, and cocaine. It's very easy to fall into this trap. In some situations, people will offer you free drinks and tokes, which can help you relax. Depending on your personality, you don't necessarily have to abstain totally, but it's very dangerous to depend on this stuff, so be careful. Besides the obvious problem of addiction, some entertainers I've known have turned to drugs as an excuse. They tell themselves, "I failed because I was drunk," so they don't have to think, "I failed because I'm not good enough."

Keep at it. It should get easier each time you play for an audience. Eventually you'll have made every mistake possible and you'll have experienced every sort of trouble. You may forget the lyrics or belch when you open your mouth to sing. Some kid may steal the money from your tip jar. Certainly the PA will die on you a few times. You'll break scores of strings and your capo may even fly off in the middle of a solo. You could easily put a capo on the fifth fret and start playing on the first fret. A drunk may lurch up and grab your microphone to sing a chorus. All this has happened to me.

The most interesting diversion of my career was when an inebriated man started bumping and grinding against my mic stand and making provocative eyes at me. Luckily, I had had about 20 years of playing experience at the time and was able to make the most of the situation. I made suggestive movements with my guitar neck, and the audience loved it (the guy did too, but I don't want to go there). You have to keep your sense of humor and see each mistake or surprise as a learning experience and/or adventure.

Be honest with yourself. Try to hear and see yourself as a stranger. Work to improve your weaknesses but don't beat your head against a wall. For example, if you have a reedy voice, you probably can't sing Delta-style blues (a truth I've had to face). Be honest about your appearance as well. If you look stupid in a certain kind of hat, don't wear it.

And be honest in how you are acting off stage with regard to your career. It's interesting how people set themselves up for failure. I've known musicians who get sick before every important gig or recording session. They can't go ahead because they have a fever or some other ailment. The fever is real, but you have to figure there's a psychological connection if it always happens at just the right moment. I knew one singer who would always get in a big fight with her accompanist, the club owner, the sound person, or the recording engineer. It was a case of, "I can't play there—that club owner was holding out on us," or, "My guitar player isn't good enough." Now, these kinds of things *can* happen, but looking for things to get angry or frustrated over can be an easy way of avoiding a challenge.

SUZANNE VEGA'S FIRST GIG

Suzanne Vega's first real gig as a solo performer was on January 2, 1976, she says with characteristic precision. "I played for a half hour at the Pit coffeehouse on 86th Street and West End Avenue. It was a church basement, and some of my friends from school came down. This was, I think, the first gig I'd ever gotten on my own, where I actually sang a lot of my own songs.

"I felt incredibly nervous, and I sang really loudly because I was afraid no one would hear me. So I sort of shouted everything and then came off stage. It was OK." Vega tried to talk a bit between songs, but she was so nervous that she wound up mostly giggling.

In the intervening years, Vega has come to love performing. "It's one of my favorite things, because it's a real challenge," she says. "I like to make the audience laugh, and I like to surprise them. I've come to really enjoy the showmanship aspects of it."

As for talking to the audience, she says, "I find if I don't do that, the whole thing just sits there. With songs like mine, you need a way in. You can't just sit there and sing them and expect people to be grateful [*laughs*]. I try to make sense to the audience; I tell them where I'm from . . . These are not your best friends, this is not your family, they don't know you. I'm telling them things about myself that I think would be interesting for them to know, and it's in story form. It does change from night to night, but it's usually a variation on a theme."

Finally, Vega offers these three lessons about performing:

Don't giggle so much.

Use your microphone well. "The microphone is on; you don't need to shout unless you want to."

Don't be resentful of the audience. "I think I used to feel angry at the audience for looking at me, because I was very shy and not very comfortable with myself. And I've learned that you can't do that; if someone is looking at you, if they've paid money to see you, then you'd better put on a show and not sit there and be morose."

—Jeffrey Pepper Rodgers

FINDING VENUES

So with all this advice in mind, you'll need a plan of attack. You have some experience playing for friends and family. What's the next step? How do you actually start life as a professional musician? I can think of three good places to start.

Senior centers. These places are always looking for entertainment and will sometimes even pay a small fee. Playing these venues is also a decent thing to do. Older folks in our society are often lonely, neglected and bored. As such they can be a great audience, especially if you have a repertoire of songs from the swing era.

Though these gigs are easy to get and the pay is low or nonexistent, you owe it to yourself and your audience to take them seriously. That means you'll have to do some preparation. First prepare a set list of about 45 minutes of music. A lot of players tape this list to the upper bout of their guitars so they can refer to it at a glance. (I've had a whimsical fantasy for a number of years of creating a miniature computer, called the Folk-Mate Select-o-Matic, with a song database that attaches to that spot.) It's a good idea to set up a small table to the side with a set list (if it's not on your guitar), a large glass of water, and a watch, since it's very uncool to glance at your wrist while you're playing.

When preparing your list, keep in mind that your set should flow. A few obvious things to avoid are too many pieces in a row in the same key or at the same tempo. As you get more experienced, you might rely less on the set list and be more prone to winging it by trying out requests or even improvising a blues on the spot. I once heard an entertainer improvise a talking blues that summarized his life story and brought him to that moment on stage. Sometimes at 2 A.M. in the fourth set you'll need to do this sort of thing to keep yourself interested. But at least have a set list to fall back on.

Open mic nights. Some of these are audition nights, others just an open stage. In the '60s and early '70s, these were really common venues for folkies. In the San Francisco Bay Area, for example, it was possible to hit an open mic every night, even if you were limited to public transportation. During the big comedy boom of the mid-'70s, all sorts of small clubs converted to comedy. A comedian could find an open mic every night, but it was harder for a musician. Now acoustic music open mics are back. They're great training grounds. You learn to work with a PA system—sometimes a very good one—and meet performers, which can be very supportive. You are usually allowed only two or three songs, so you really have to make an immediate impact. Remember you can ease into the scene by just going to watch and listen a few times.

Street singing. This is a great way to get your feet wet (literally as well as figuratively). To be successful, you have to grab people's attention quickly and hold it. The best street entertainers have a killer ten- to 15-minute act that includes a lot of clever reminders to "feed the kitty." A disadvantage that this route shares with the open mic is that you don't learn the rhythm of the 45-minute set, which is a must for moving up to the next level.

You can actually make quite a bit of money working the streets, and in some ways it's easier than being on stage. People aren't supposed to be listening, so if they don't pay any attention, you don't get the feeling that you lost an audience. On the other hand, you have to be able to grab them. Hundreds of people passing you by without a glance can be depressing. And unless you play and sing really loudly, you'll need to invest some money in amplification equipment.

As you start to get comfortable playing in the streets, at open mics, in old folks' homes, and/or for friends, you can start to try for more gigs. Little coffeehouses and bars where you pass the hat or jar are a good bet. Sometimes you can even talk a local joint into trying some entertainment.

GUITAR CAREERS

Q *I'm fresh out of high school and taking a couple of years off to hone my guitar skills. I was wondering if you could give me a little advice as to how to get started as a guitar player. I play in cafés and at benefits, but my town just isn't all that musical. What town should I bum around in to be discovered? Nashville? San Francisco? Los Angeles?*

A The first thing you should realize is that bumming around any town is not the way to pursue a musical career. It takes hard work and a strong commitment to your art to make a living in the music business. The competition is as fierce and plentiful as it has ever been. Moving to a "music town" will just increase the competition. You may not feel that your town is particularly musical, but it's all too easy to become infected with the "grass is always greener" syndrome. Prince, R.E.M., and Nirvana all managed to do pretty well staying put in their respective hometowns of Minneapolis, Athens, and Seattle.

Try to stay where you are and build up your audience. Book as many gigs as you can, start a mailing list, set up a Web site, put out a self-produced CD or tape, and learn how to promote yourself. Then increase your home turf by going on the road, at first to places you can drive to easily. Take a look at a map and see how many towns are within a two- or three-hour drive. Get gigs in this area. Booking agents, managers, and record companies want to see that an artist is able to make a big splash in a small pond before committing time and money.

The good news is that you're young. Sleeping on floors and surviving on beans and rice is somehow much easier to endure before your hair starts turning gray. If you're committed to making music your life's work, you won't care. And the rewards will be worth it. Plenty of musicians live satisfying lives pursuing their art in a small but meaningful and self-supporting way. They never get "discovered." And they are often better off for it.

—Scott Nygaard

This brings up a whole other aspect of the business, the importance of personal relationships with club owners, booking agents, and other musicians. Club owners and bookers are primarily concerned with how good you are and how many butts you can put in the seats, but they also care about how reliable you are and how easy you are to get along with. This is especially true when they have to choose an opening act for a headliner. Other musicians will be more likely to play with you or ask you to fill in for them if you have developed a personal rapport.

CREATING AN IDENTITY

You should begin to think about exactly what image you're trying to get across. In show business, you sell yourself as a total package. Ideally you want people to be interested in you before you open your mouth or move your fingers. Your look should reflect your sound, unless the contrast is the point of it all. Most of this is pretty obvious. For example, if you're performing Porter, Gershwin, and Ellington tunes, you don't want to go on stage in a pair of overalls. A cowboy hat creates a certain look, a fedora another, and a jockey cap another. A black cocktail dress conveys a certain image, a shaved head and body piercings another. Your image should be comfortable, probably a somewhat exaggerated version of yourself.

A lot of the greatest entertainers in the folk world have been able to create wonderful personas that they live both on and off the stage. Elliott Adnopoz, a doctor's son from Brooklyn, successfully reinvented himself as Ramblin' Jack Elliott. U. Utah Phillips, the Golden Voice of the Great Southwest, is a wonderful character with his endless stories, Model T Ford truck, watch chain, and fedora. I've met both these guys and can tell you they essentially are these characters. It makes their stage show that much stronger and their fan base that much larger.

You can even use a stage name. It can be liberating because the stage "you" isn't carrying around all your baggage. You could relate this to tribal cultures where folks have a "real" name, an everyday name, and a war name. On a lower-brow level you could relate it to comic-book superheroes. Sure, Bruce Wayne can't sing a lick, but that Batman can really get down.

Some entertainers are held back by never getting their identity right. They may even choose the wrong presentation on purpose at some level—it's that fear-of-success bugaboo again. Most of us start off by mimicking someone else's look, but you have to learn what works and is unique for you (although there is money in being an Elvis clone, I suppose). Certain licks you play, poses you strike, or expressions you use will work. One song will sound great after song A but lousy after song B.

Experiment with how much you talk. Between-song chatter is traditional and even expected in the folk world, but it can be overdone. How much you talk depends on the venue and your own personality and abilities. In a noisy bar you'll sound stupid telling the history of how you wrote a particular song, but on songwriters' night at a coffeehouse such a story could work perfectly. Some people really have the gift of gab; others don't. Be honest with yourself and tailor your act accordingly.

One trap almost all beginning performers fall into is apologizing all the time. I've heard comments like "The dressing room is cold so my hands don't work," or "Here's a song I'm still learning," or "I haven't changed my strings in a year" hundreds of times, and they always bug me. I still catch myself doing it, though, and when I do I usually apologize for apologizing.

Humor can work well. Actually, quite a few comedians started as musicians (including Jack Benny and the Smothers Brothers) and found out that their patter was going over better than their playing, or their look was just making people laugh. A few corny jokes while you're tuning or just to loosen things up can work quite well. A lightweight comment after a serious song can work, but don't overdo it and send too many mixed signals to an audience.

As a practical matter, you should develop clever methods of mentioning your tip jar if you have one out. You can talk over some blues changes: "Thanks for listening. I'm Jane Doe. Don't forget the tip jar." You could write a song to encourage tipping: "I've rambled near and far / Living on money from the old tip jar." Having a "plant" in the audience conspicuously throw in a large bill is a good gambit.

Another good practical idea is to start a mailing list. When you play somewhere, leave out a sheet of paper or little cards people can write their street and e-mail addresses on. Then for future gigs you can send out postcards and/or e-mails. Some entertainers send out chatty newsletters every month ("I've been working on my new CD, which should be out in June. My cat knocked over the Christmas tree. My cousin Fred just had a head transplant operation and looks much better"). Modern computer database software makes printing postcard labels a breeze. I advise against getting a mailing permit. Stamped postcards are cheaper and much more reliable than letters sent that way. Obviously, e-mail communication is a great way to go. With e-mail, by the way, I highly recommend sending to your list with the bcc (blind carbon copy) function so that your entire list isn't visible to every member on it. This is good manners and good business. By the way, getting on other musicians' mailing lists is a good way to find new places to play, though you should pay them back by going to some of their gigs and/or passing on venues you discover.

That's the heart of what I've learned in the performance business. Put all this advice together, and with some work and luck you can be a professional guitarist. Of course, I've never managed to become a big star, so if you make it, let me know what I've left out.

Performing Tips and Tactics

Kristina Olsen

Kristina Olsen gets into the groove.

Back in 1985, I took a performing workshop from Gamble Rogers in Texas in the middle of the day in the middle of summer. The heat treated us like cookies in the oven; we melted, changed shape, and lost our form, and I couldn't imagine how I would be able to concentrate on what he was going to say. I can still remember the dust and the heat waves, and years later I can still remember nearly verbatim the words he spoke. He changed my life as a performer.

The first thing that Rogers said was, "You owe your audience everything. Your audience has just given you their most precious gift, the gift of their time, and you owe them everything for that." Everything else he said that day reinforced that statement. Rogers was a wizard of a performer, and he always gave his audience that kind of respect. I'll recount as much as I can of what he said about preparing for a performance, and I'll add other tips I've gleaned from watching countless performers succeed and fail, and from the countless times that I've succeeded and failed myself. Then I'll turn to ways to keep your audience interested once you're in the midst of your gig.

VARY YOUR SET

When you build your set, you need to remember that one minute on the stage for you is like an hour to an audience. They are sitting in a chair that is getting more uncomfortable by the moment, so don't play songs in the same key or with the same rhythm back to back. The audience will know intellectually that they are hearing two different songs, but subconsciously they will think it is one long, boring piece. It is easy to lull the audience into a trance. You must break up the keys and the tempos to prevent that. Playing more than one instrument is a great way to sonically vary the show. You can also vary your show by playing in different styles and at different volume levels. Break up the music with funny stories and end with your strongest song. Hey, you want an encore, don't you?

Keep your sets short. Leave your audience wanting more. If you are an opener, this goes quadruple. If you want to sell a lot of CDs or cassettes, do a short, tight show. This can be a difficult rule to follow because it is so fun to be on stage that we would stay there all week if given the chance.

PRACTICE IN POSITION

When you practice playing your instrument, practice in the position that you perform in. That means always using a strap or sitting in a chair that's the same height. I know many people who play sitting down at home and can't figure out why they flop when they go to the gig and play standing up. Your muscles memorize tiny movements when you play. If you shift your position, you use different muscle patterns and your body feels like it has never played the piece before. In general, it is a good idea to perform standing up. It gives the show more energy, you breathe better (which gives you more energy), and in most venues it means that your audience can see you better.

LOOK 'EM IN THE EYE

Eye contact is one of the best ways to connect with an audience. It feels great to close your eyes, especially when you are singing a vulnerable song, but when you're able to open your eyes and sing directly to your audience, they feel the vulnerability, and the connection is much stronger. On songs with more of an angry edge, the eye contact shows that you are not frightened of what you're saying. Most performers will look at their hands or their instrument throughout the piece when they don't need to look. Their hands know exactly where to go on their own, but the muscles have also memorized that turn of the head to go along with the finger moves. It feels like a whole new piece when you play it without moving your head. Looking at the instrument is a way to avoid the awkwardness of looking at the audience, but eye contact is what the audience craves. They want you to sing to them.

A great exercise is to join up with another performer and play songs for each other without ever breaking eye contact. This is a very scary and sensuous exercise. The person who is listening must also not break eye contact.

PLAY OPEN MICS

I still go to open mics to try out new humor and new songs. I make a special point of listening to the other acts at each open mic. It is great to watch other performers and monitor your mood throughout their shows. It is pretty much the only school of performing that we have. Most of the audience members at an open mic are performers, and you won't help your career much by talking through their sets and bolting for the door as soon as you're done playing. Open mics are difficult performing situations because no one is really there to hear you. This provides you with an excellent challenge: if you can get this audience to listen and respond to you, you have really succeeded in performing.

Many of the best performers interject funny spoken parts between their pieces. Not only do they give their audience the incredible gift of laughter, but they break up the somnambulistic state of mind that music can induce. You say, "But I'm not funny." Almost every performer has at one point in his or her career done something that really cracked the audience up. The way I started getting funny parts into my shows was by memorizing things I said by accident that made the audience laugh.

Open mics are a great place to try different things out, kind of like a performance lab. You don't want to test bits in your one really big show. That is where you use all the stuff that you know works. So, at your lab gig, when you hear the audience laugh, make a mental note of it. Think about it when you are off stage. Why did they laugh? Try it out in another lab show. Did they laugh again? If they did, can you take the laugh further? Can you make it more funny? It's a lot like editing a song you have just written. You keep stripping it down to the bare essence. Too many details confuse the audience; you only want the information that is building your laugh.

PREP YOUR GUITAR

Get to the concert site early so that your instruments and strings can acclimate and won't be in a state of flux while you are on stage. Figure out how long strings last for you and make sure your strings are at their peak for your show. My strings last for about a week of performing and are at their best after I've played on them for about an hour. I have many friends who have to change their strings for every performance. Do you use electronic equipment? Christine Lavin changes her batteries before every single show because she never wants to have battery problems on stage. She takes her audience's time very seriously.

Kristina Olsen with cellist Peter Grayling.

Do you break strings on stage? Steve Goodman was incredible at turning a tune into a wild improvisational string rap as he changed the broken string and then slipping seamlessly back into the tune where he left off. It left his audience breathless with excitement. If you do break strings, have a spare guitar on stage ready to go or be practiced at entertaining your audience as you change the string. (Most musicians practice only the pieces they are going to play; you can and should practice your *performance* as well.)

Do you change tunings? Some performers have a spare guitar for altered tunings. David Wilcox, who changes tunings on virtually every song, has memorized the distance the gear must move to get to the new tuning. He retunes the strings while the audience is applauding. He can't hear a thing; he's just memorized how far to turn the gears. Then, when the audience is finished clapping, he can check and fine-tune his strings in an instant without wasting his audience's time. It's incredible how accurate that is. We musicians don't think twice about the fact that we have memorized extremely precise movements of our hands on the fingerboard, like jumping six frets in a millisecond without looking, but how many of us ever thought about memorizing the detuning of a string?

START STRONG

The start of your show is so important. You want to let your audience know that you are a competent performer and that you are going to take care of them. Audiences are very nervous for us. Most of the audience can't understand how a person could get up on a stage in front of a bunch of strangers without having a heart attack or a nervous breakdown. Start with two of your strongest pieces. Sometimes the inevitable thing happens: the mic isn't on or you lose your pick or drop your guitar. Make a gentle joke about it and get on with the show.

Generally it is best not to talk until after the second song, unless you are a comedian. It is best to take charge of the stage with what you do best, which we'll assume is playing music. Then you can have the luxury of speaking. You must earn that luxury. When you are speaking to an audience, you are still taking their time, so your patter must enhance your show. It must either be funny or poignant or give the audience special information about a tune. Don't be self-indulgent on stage. You must look at every second you take on that stage and ask if you are wasting your audience's time or enhancing the show.

Take notice of your surroundings. During the show you can make some comment about the concert venue or the city—something that tells the audience you know where you are. An audience's sense of self is tied into the place they live, and nobody wants someone from out of town to come and crank out the exact same show they just did last week in Perth or bash the place they live in. You can gently tease the audience about something, but always include a positive comment. Once, when I was playing in a small club in Australia, I noticed that there were locks on the outside of the ladies' toilets. I had fun teasing the audience about that, but I also made sure to mention the incredible natural beauty surrounding the town.

LEO KOTTKE ON STAGE RAP

The first time I spoke on stage, I had been playing for almost three years quite regularly in Minneapolis. I would sit up there and play, but I couldn't even look the audience in the eye, and I couldn't talk—I just played and sang. One night while battling with a gooseneck mic stand, I remembered a time on the farm when we were trying to kill a chicken that just wouldn't die. I said, out of the blue, "Has anybody here ever killed a chicken?"—before I could stop myself or become self-conscious about it—and they laughed. I laughed, too, and then I couldn't stop talking about it because it just cracked me up. I told the whole story, how we finally backed the tractor over the thing, and how it was still kicking with the tractor on it. We just had to walk away and leave it there. After the set, the club owner, Mike Justin, was furious. He said, "Do you know how many songs you just played? Two!" It was a 45-minute set and I had talked for 40 minutes! Then he said, "And it wasn't funny!"

So I went from sheer terror to sheer babble, and I had to come back in the other direction. But I did find that you could really lighten the load and that it was fun talking to an audience. You could set up the tunes. When it really works, it's like a bunch of little launching pads, not so much for each tune but for the layers of a set.

MAKE 'EM BREATHE

You are full of adrenaline on stage, and your brain is full of oxygen, especially if you are singing or playing a wind instrument. Meanwhile, your audience is slumped in chairs barely breathing at all. Oxygen is like a big dose of healthy uppers. You need to get your audience to breathe deeply. Unless you are playing in parts of California that are ripe with crystals and aura fresheners, your audience will not appreciate your telling them to breathe deeply. Your audience is made up of a bunch of healthy individualists who don't like being told what to do, even if you are right and it is good for them. So you have to trick them.

Two great ways to get your audience to breathe deeply is to get them to laugh or to get them to sing along. I was watching Jesse Winchester years ago in a small club. I love his stuff, but partway through the show I realized that I was getting tired and the chair was getting uncomfortable. I was just thinking that I might leave early when he did a wild dance that was very funny. I must have laughed really hard, because I suddenly felt full of energy, and, miraculously enough, the chair was no longer uncomfortable.

Sing-alongs are tricky because most audiences hate the idea of them until they are actually singing (except audiences in New England and Old England, who will sing along on songs without choruses that they have never heard before). Even if you don't have any singing in your act, you can get the audience to make some sound at a particular part of a tune. Getting audience members involved is like giving them a job. They may resent you for it for a moment, but by the end of the show they will get a boost in self-esteem from being a part of your show and doing the job well.

All of the funny stories that have become nearly memorized bits in my show started out as me just telling my audience what happened to me that day, letting them know that I liked their town and that I wasn't doing the exact same show I did in Antwerp. When I got a laugh, I started the very slow process of memorizing the laughs and distilling it all down. Now those stories are as requested as my songs. There are stories about Alaska, Seattle, Australia, and Scotland. They aren't memorized, but I have memorized where the laughs are. I call the laughs my fence posts. I just tell the audience very conversationally what I was doing that day. The words and phrases vary, but when I get to the fence posts, they are always the same; they have been worked over meticulously for timing and phrasing.

Never introduce a funny story or joke with, "This is very funny" or "I have something very funny to tell you." That audience full of mavericks will show that they are individuals by refusing to laugh. And don't laugh at your own punch lines or jokes. You can laugh naturally before you start, as if you were remembering something funny, but punch lines work best if you sound like you're just trying to tell the story. The audience will laugh, but you keep on telling the story, like you have an urgent need to get it off your chest. If you pause for the audience to laugh, they will know this is a staged bit and will go into maverick mode again.

In the same vein, don't tell the audience what they are about to experience. I've seen so many songwriters introduce a song by telling the audience exactly what is going to happen in it. By the time they hear the song, the audience is bored. Your introductions must be entertaining on their own, or they must be intriguing so the audience listens harder to the song.

When you perform, you create a persona that ultimately should be as true to who you really are as possible. If you are fake, the audience will sense that and not be nearly as engaged in your show as they could be. In the same vein, when you are performing, be in the song or piece; don't be thinking about the next song. That's how you forget lyrics and put on a flat show.

STAGE FRIGHT

I know few performers who haven't experienced crippling stage fright at one time or another. Ironically, the best cure for stage fright is to perform often. I think your body eventually gets tired of going into hyper fight-or-flight adrenaline mode and starts to calm down. If you are going to do a big show and you really suffer from stage fright, do a bunch of little shows or open mics before the big date to get your body acclimated. Other than that, be really well prepared for your show. You need a strong foundation to hold you up there. And *breathe deeply!* Breathing gives you the oxygen you need to deliver a peak performance, and taking deep regular breaths will calm you down.

THANKS BUT NO APOLOGIES

Always give songwriters credit when you perform their songs. Acknowledge band members, sound and light people, promoters, the musicians who are on the bill with you, and the audience. People love to be mentioned. You can break this up so you don't have a long list of thanks; scatter them throughout the show.

Don't apologize. If you are collected and prepared for your show, you shouldn't have anything to apologize for. If things go wrong, once again, deal with it with grace and humor and let the audience know through your poise that you are fine. They didn't give up their time and money to hear you apologize.

BE TACTFUL WITH TALKERS

Never blame an audience for anything. If they are talking through your set, either you are not interesting enough for them or you booked the wrong gig. I have seen performers tell audiences to be quiet. Oof, the audience hates that. That will throw your show right off. When people are talking and making noise, the first thing I do is use dynamics. The natural instinct is to get louder to cover up the talking, but that usually just encourages the talkers to start yelling. I'll play a loud song and then bring it way down suddenly. All you can hear is the person talking for a second before they get self-conscious and start whispering. I do this a few times until they get tired of trying to talk over the roller coaster and shut up. I make sure that the loud and soft parts of my piece are appropriate to the song I'm playing. The 95 percent of the audience that is listening doesn't need to have the show ruined because of the 5 percent that isn't listening. It's hard to remember when some people are making noise that there are a whole lot of people really listening. Don't punish them by trying to punish the noisy ones or by doing a half-assed show. The audience is still giving you its time, and you owe them the best show you can give.

Usually an audience that pays an admission price will want to get its money's worth by listening. If you are playing a bar or a university lunchroom where no one paid to get in, the audience will assume that you have no worth and usually won't listen. Many of them went there specifically to talk to someone. Still, these venues can be lab gigs where you try out your performances. If you get a nonpaying audience to listen, you have really done something.

On the other hand, if you are in an audience listening to a performer and some bozo is talking, go over and ask them to be quiet. Audience members get to do that. The performer that you are listening to will silently say a thousand thanks, as will the rest of the audience. By the same token, if you've just finished your set and the next act is on, you must be absolutely quiet. If you have a bunch of fans who want to talk to you, either suggest to them that you leave the room to talk or wait until the next intermission. I can't tell you how often I've been at a gig and the only noise was from the performer who just got off stage.

Always earn your encores. I've seen performers tell an audience to give them an encore. Either the listeners refuse or they comply but resent the performer for asking. This is also true when it comes to standing ovations. Even if you word your request humorously, the audience still ends up resenting you.

Believe it or not, sometimes the best gift we have is having small, uninterested audiences in the beginning of our careers. We get to test our wings with people who are only half paying attention to our awkward flappings and crash landings. When we do something so unique and spectacular that the disinterested stop their conversations and turn and listen to us, we know that we have something that will be useful when we are playing to 2,000 people.

Memorizing and Mental Preparation

Sharon Isbin

One of the big challenges of performing composed music is learning the music well enough that you can communicate it clearly and effortlessly in front of an audience—so your eyes are not glued to the score, and you can relax and connect with the emotional meaning of what you're playing. Let's look at some effective techniques that will help you translate a piece of music from the page to the stage.

Classical guitar master Sharon Isbin.

LEARNING AND VISUALIZING

The more you understand the language and structure of a piece, the easier it will be to memorize. The same is true with any form of learning that involves complex thought patterns. We've all had the experience at one time or another, for example, of trying to memorize poetry or lines from a play. The ease or difficulty of that process is determined by one's understanding of the emotional, historical, personal, and structural context of what an author is expressing. If you perceive the text as merely unrelated individual words or sentences, or as unintelligible sounds (as in a foreign language), the brain has little incentive to retain it. However, if you understand the words and integrate them within a logical pattern of thought, memorizing becomes much easier.

Similarly, one's ability to remember a musical score is enhanced by a clear understanding of the phrasing and the melodic, rhythmic, and harmonic structure of the work. Before learning a piece, write out phrasing marks so that the structural units are clear. Indicate both small and large units of phrasing, and outline the large structure as well. Identify important harmonic landmarks and modulations. Add right- and left-hand fingerings that best express the phrasing, voicing, counterpoint, desired articulation, and chosen timbre. Then practice the music phrase by phrase and section by section.

When you can play the music by heart, put away the guitar and visualize the left-hand (and eventually the right-hand) finger patterns, section by section. If you have trouble playing without the score before you've done the mental work, then introduce visualization earlier. When a finger or fret is not clear, refer to the score. I prefer to visualize the fingers, frets, and strings rather than actual notes, because these are the final images sent by the brain before a sound is produced. As you visualize the right- and left-hand fingerings, hear the music in your mind exactly as you wish it to sound. This means hearing it with your ideal phrasing, rhythm, articulation, dymanics, tempo, and expression (including any rubato, ritards, etc.). At first, have the score handy to correct and rehearse any sections that are not clear; you may also have to work fast passages up to tempo gradually.

While you're doing this, it's important that you don't get so focused on individual passages that you lose sight of the big picture. Mentally coordinate the visualization of your left-hand fingers with the sound of the notes, hear the notes within the context of a phrase, and study the relationship of individual phrases to each other and to the rhythmic, melodic, and harmonic structure of the entire piece. In addition to learning individual details of a work, you must unite and integrate them into a continuum of thought that has direction and purpose. If you form a large frame of reference built solidly on structural components, a single glitch won't derail you, because you'll know exactly where the piece is heading.

This combined method of analysis, motor repetition, and visualization increases not only the speed of memorization but also its solidity and staying power.

REMEMBERING THE WORDS

Q *How do the pros remember all the words to the songs on their set lists?*

A There are many ways to memorize words. Some people have a sort of photographic memory and can remember what the lyrics looked like on the page. Others remember the story; for example, in a long ballad, they remember that the fair maiden has to meet the young soldier before she can ask him to marry her.

Usually, if you have the order of events in your head and have sung the song often enough looking at the words, you'll remember them in performance. Writing the words out over and over is another way to memorize them.

If you are an occasional performer, part of the problem may be that you're just not playing the song often enough. Touring musicians are usually singing the active songs in their repertoire three to five times a week. If you ask them to sing an older song that they haven't performed in a while, you'll often find that they have trouble with the words the first time through.

Memory is a muscle that gets better with use. If your brain knows that the words are available if you just open your eyes and look down at the paper in front of you, then it won't work very hard. When you're practicing a song, put the words out of sight and force yourself to get through it. Skip over the parts you don't remember, but get all the way to the end. Then when you're done, look at the parts you didn't remember and try it again.

—Cosy Sheridan

PREPARING FOR A CONCERT

In order to be relaxed and confident, it is essential to be well prepared long before the concert. Learn the music fluently and conscientiously as much in advance as possible. Once you have learned a piece, rehearse it from start to finish to explore the full range of musical expression and to develop the requisite physical and mental stamina. You may still need to isolate sections to address specific technical challenges.

Pace yourself so that you can visualize the entire program flawlessly, without the aid of scores, at least ten days before the concert. During the week prior to the concert, continue to rehearse the program with this visualization technique each day. This approach, because it is unhampered by the technical difficulties of an instrument, also allows you to develop and expand your musical goals and vision.

When you feel confident with each piece, practice playing through the entire program. You should do this daily at least ten days before a concert to develop stamina. Work on individual pieces additionally when necessary. And it is an invaluable experience to play through your program informally for others.

It is also helpful to practice some form of relaxation or meditation on a regular basis. I have done transcendental meditation since age 17, and it has been a wonderful way for me to reduce stress, reinforce memory and concentration, and expand musical expression. On the day of a concert, I follow my daily routine of meditating once in the morning for 20 minutes and then again in the afternoon. You can also introduce positive suggestions while in this trancelike state, because the mind is especially receptive. As in autohypnosis, however, only suggest ideas that are believable and realistic, and don't drill.

Replacing negative thoughts about performance with positive ones can be as simple as reprogramming a computer. There is no reason to allow irrational demons—conscious or subconscious—to dominate your thinking or undermine your self-confidence.

If you have prepared effectively, there is little more to do the day of a concert than warm up with a few scales and exercises and run through the program very softly, saving your energy for the performance. You might also wish to play fast passages under tempo. Rest and relax after practicing, have a good meal about three hours before, and warm up again just before the performance. Then go for it!

RELAXING ON STAGE

If you have effectively prepared for a performance but still feel tense on stage, you might consider the question of musical and spiritual immersion. Are you really listening to the music you play? The more you are engaged musically, the less time you will have to be nervous or distracted. Are you actively feeling the music, emotionally and spiritually? If not, your subconscious could be saying, "This whole process is a big lie, and I don't really care what happens."

After all, you have to believe in what you are doing in order to be effective, and that is possible only when you are giving it your heart and soul. You must be able to identify with and feel the music you are playing. And remember to emote in the practice room, because that is what allows your feelings to be free and open on stage.

If the issue for you is not musical or emotional, then perhaps it is psychological. One can have the best intentions and make excellent preparations but still suffer from irrational fears that block the flow of positive energy. Sometimes these fears were once realistic and legitimate and have carried over from earlier days when you didn't really know how to prepare effectively. With effort and determination, you can deprogram these gremlins and replace them with positive, believable thoughts. Self-hypnosis and repetitive writing can be helpful in this quest to be more in control of your conscious and subconscious patterns of thinking.

MAKING FACES

Q *My teacher has told me to stop making faces when I play. How important is this?*

A If your facial gestures are genuine and natural expressions of mood and feeling, they can be an organic part of your performance. More often than not, however, facial grimaces are a product of tension and reflect awkward hand motions and strained technique. Such gestures only worsen overall tension and call attention to a player's discomfort. They can even fragment phrasing and impede legato playing since both require relaxed technique. When facial tension affects throat and ear muscles, breathing and hearing become constricted.

The visual impact of strange facial expressions is also terribly distracting for an audience. It's hard to take players seriously when their tongues are sticking out or they appear ready to sneeze at any moment! When in doubt, videotape your playing and see for yourself. The bottom line: if the image is not compatible with the music, it will detract from the performance. Practice with attention to relaxing your lips, jaw, tongue, eyebrows, ears, and neck. The natural emotive expressions will then emerge.

—Sharon Isbin

Making Stage Fright Work for You

John Herndon

Remember that tune by the Band called "Stage Fright"? They named a whole album after it—for good reason. I've known some people who have it really bad. We've all heard of famous actors who have an unvarying routine before going on stage—throwing up.

Performance anxiety. Everyone gets it, or 99 percent of us, anyway. It's what keeps most parlor pickers, even very good ones, from discovering the joy of performing for an audience. The rush of adrenaline—the fight-or-flight hormone—that comes when you step on stage can make your knees quake. But it's really useful stuff, energy you can put into your performance.

A long time ago I learned a little secret from an experienced performer about dealing with stage fright—even making it work for me. That nervousness you feel is the energy of the audience's expectations. All those pairs of eyes are pumping the energy right into you. If you're not ready, it can blow you away, just like overloading a fuse. But if you recognize it for what it is, you can let it flow through you and right back to the audience. You can act like an amplifier and transmitter and send it back to the audience in the form of a high-energy performance. That may not be very scientific advice (my mentor was an old hippie), but it works for me.

There are two important things to bear in mind about that audience. One, they are willing participants in the performance. Ever notice how an audience at a comedy show will laugh at lines that aren't funny? The same is true of an audience for a musical performance. They want you to succeed. And two, they're people just like you. They put their pants on one leg at a time.

John Herndon on mandolin.

With that in mind, you can employ a few simple techniques to help you handle all that energy. Probably the most important thing you can do is be prepared. Know your material thoroughly. Since the excitement of being on stage may reduce your abilities as a player by about 20 percent, plan to include in your set only licks that you know you can hit. Competence breeds confidence.

When you're waiting to go on, focus on your material—not on yourself. The cult of personality that springs up around performers notwithstanding, the performance is not really about you. It's about the music. Instead of worrying about what others think of your haircut or the cut of your clothes, concentrate on the music. Silently rehearse the lyrics and chord changes. Just like a golfer or gymnast, you can previsualize your performance, and this can go a long way toward helping you relax. Of course, in your visualization the audience loves you and you get a huge, heartfelt ovation.

Teach your body to relax. It helps to keep yourself in reasonable physical shape. When you have good cardiovascular conditioning, your heart rate and blood pressure stay low under stress, and you're more efficient at breathing. And breathing is essential. Before your performance, take a few deep breaths. These are full, cleansing breaths that you feel in your belly. Don't forget to exhale thoroughly, from the pit of your stomach.

Try to find a moment for quiet centering. Even if you're sitting at a table in the audience waiting for your turn to take the mic, you can close your eyes as you take a few deep breaths. Again, even in a crowded room, you can do natural relaxation exercises and no one will notice. Start with your feet and work your way up through your calves, thighs, buttocks, abdomen, back, hands and arms, shoulders, neck and face, alternately tensing the muscles and relaxing them. For example, sitting comfortably with your feet on the floor, tense your feet, then relax. Now tense your calves, and relax. Keep it up until you've tensed and relaxed all your body parts. You can do this while you visualize your successful performance. And keep breathing.

Actors sometimes employ the following mental technique in preparation for taking the stage. Imagine that you are in a box, the smallest box you can possibly fit into. Make your body as tiny as you possibly can so you take up the least possible room. Now turn it around. You are in a huge space. Expand yourself to take up all that room. Feel your head reaching toward the ceiling. This practice seems to warm and stretch the muscles of your imagination, and that allows you to project the feeling of the song to the farthest corner of the room.

Next thing you know, it's your turn to go on. No time to be scared. When you take the stage, your spirit fills the room. Remember to stand up straight and keep breathing. Hit that kick-off, strike up the band, and sing out. They love you!

Troubleshooting Your Show

Mike Barris

Mike Barris plays the Turtle Hill Folk Festival.

You're playing your first folk festival. You stride onto the stage, eager to raise a few eyebrows with your guitar artistry, but the crowd is still under the spell of the preceding act, who turned the place into a church with her tranquil love songs. You launch into an upbeat tune; a number of people, put off by you, collect their lawn chairs and leave (heading for the nearby barn dance). In a bid to stop the exodus, you rachet up the energy level, but you snap an E string. What's going on?

As anyone who plays out regularly can tell you, making a performance go smoothly is no cinch. Once you've experienced the incredible high that comes with clicking with an audience, you're hooked; every outing becomes a quest to have the crowd eating out of your hand. But even the world's best performers can have their hands full navigating the stormy ocean of variables that make it hard for things to go right. The character of the performance space, the mood of the audience, the temperament of the performer—these are just a few of the tangible and intangible elements you have to deal with to make your show go off with as few hitches as possible. OK, so you can't control every problem, but here are a few suggestions to help along the way.

SOLVE PROBLEMS IN REHEARSAL

An amazing number of performers think nothing of subjecting an audience to an on-stage rehearsal. "I just learned this song this afternoon, so excuse me for using the sheet music," they say. That's unfair, when you consider that people in the audience have gone to the trouble to shower, change clothes, and drive down to a club to see you play. The fact is, audiences who have paid good money for entertainment will write you off quickly if you don't deliver the goods right away. So before you apply for your first job at the local folk club, identify the technical issues, chords, or lyrics that are giving you trouble. Set goals for addressing these things, and be systematic—don't practice with the TV on. Then try out your material in a low-risk environment such as an open stage. Observe what does/doesn't work. Tape yourself (audio and video). Review the tape: Do you look comfortable? Do your wardrobe and your haircut look up to date? Do you speak smoothly and succinctly? Do you display good technical chops? Do you have interesting arrangements? Do you pace the show well? Do you impress people as someone special? Also, learn from watching other performers work live. Note how he/she makes an entrance, weaves the set, raps with the crowd. In addition, pay attention to the stage-craft ideas contained in other performers' live cassettes, CDs, and videos. Record your observations in a journal.

Staying in contact with your instrument through regular practice will keep your chops sharp; you'll always be warmed up. That will help you avoid hand injuries and give you a much-needed technical edge once you get down to playing for paying customers, who will show a nervous, inexperienced prey no mercy.

INVEST IN RELIABLE EQUIPMENT

Don't scrimp where gear is concerned. You'll only increase your chances of having something break down in the middle of a gig. Generally speaking, you get what you pay for. On big-ticket items, comparison shop; after you get a price quote from one store, see if a rival store can beat it. Pack two good instrument cords, a direct box, a good microphone, two microphone cords, extra strings, a string winder, picks, tuner, batteries, wire cutters, solder and soldering iron (for emergency cord repair). Change strings frequently so they don't break. Roll up cords using the "roadie twirl"—one loop in one direction followed by a loop in the opposite direction—to extend their life.

BUILD A BIG SONG LIST

The larger your book, the greater your chances of coping with changing dynamics in the room, the hallmark of an accomplished performer. Some singer-guitarists know as many as 600 songs. Categorize your songs by tempos and tape the list to the back of the guitar. Be sure to include several crowd-pleasing tunes that you can play fairly easily while you're getting your bearings on stage.

Try to gauge in advance which songs will work best in the show. Having a rough idea of the tunes you're going to pitch to the audience will make you feel more serene at the start of the performance, giving you another edge. Try to visit the venue before the show, but if you can't, use what you already know about the club to help you sketch a set list. Does it feature original music or covers? Are you background or foreground? An opening act or a headliner? Another trick is to try to size up the space as you enter it for the first time. Do people sit far from the stage? Lie on a lawn and relax? Stroll amid food and craft booths? What songs would seem to fit the mood?

Be prepared to scrap the list if the show takes off in an unexpected direction. This list is just a guideline, anyway; the real "list" should emerge from your reading of the audience's mood as the performance progresses.

FINGERNAIL FIRST AID

Q *I tore a nail on the day of a show. What could I have done to fix it well enough to get through the gig?*

A If the nail is torn but still attached, I highly recommend the Savarez Nail Making and Repair Kit, which includes a special self-adhesive silk, resin, and applicators. Or you can affix a patch of China Silk (made by IBD, and sold in the nail-repair departments of drugstores) with Krazy Glue on the top side of the nail. In order to preserve a good tone, wait a few minutes for the glue to harden and then sand the edge with 500-grade (or finer) silicone-coated sandpaper until it is perfectly smooth.

If you lost the nail, the Savarez nail kit shows you how to build another. Or you can cut to shape a Player's Nail (made by Balcan Music and Accessories, 67-11 Yellowstone Blvd. #1C, Flushing, NY 11375)—or a Ping-Pong–ball substitute—and affix it with Krazy Glue to the underside of your nail. Again, smooth the edge with sandpaper.

Avoid soaking the mended nail in water for any significant length of time. If the nail does get wet, treat it with another dose of glue to ensure that it will remain intact during the gig.

—Sharon Isbin

USE A RANGE OF TEMPOS

Audiences will lavish you with love if you convince them that you are worth liking. Do this by using a range of tempos to stretch and warm up their so-called approval muscles. There will be times when a slow opening tune will be in order (depending on the combined atmosphere of the room, the makeup of the people in the room, and your emotional, spiritual, and physical state), but generally, it's a good idea to open with a medium-up tune. After that, welcome them to your show; now you could play a slightly more up tune, followed by a radically different medium tune. If you're not getting through to them, scan the house for someone who is patting his foot or bobbing his head in time to the music. Play to him; feed off his energy. Smile. Give back that energy to the audience.

Perhaps you could play a slow tune. By now, you should be relying less on a prepared set list and trusting the tone of the applause to tell you which songs to choose next from your master list.

You'll help your cause by allowing the performance to become easy and natural. Audiences seek entertainment to escape reality; thus the more you look and sound at home, the easier it will be to pull them into your world. Keep song intros short, but if your forte is storytelling, spin a yarn or two. If the audience's attention flags, now's the time to trot out any special instruments, sing-a-longs, or gimmicks you were saving for later. Above all, don't panic. You need to stay within yourself to use your music intelligently. Once you've established control, lay back. Enjoy yourself. Challenge them. Pushing them past their emotional limits will make them remember you.

DEVELOP PEOPLE SKILLS

Audiences are people, and when you're dealing with people, anything can happen. Unfortunately, how well you handle paying customers in particular will surely affect whether management asks you back. Generally, if trouble breaks, take a deep breath and go with the flow. If a three-year-old kid wanders onto the stage and starts dancing, play off his dance steps. Ask the audience to give it up for your "special guest." They'll eat it up. (Expect his people eventually to show up to take him off your hands.) If some clown starts blowing harp from his seat three feet from you, burst his bubble. Say, nicely, "I don't remember giving you a part in my show. You must really be desperate." If some wise guy starts calling out tunes you obviously don't play, say, "Whoops, you must have come to the wrong show tonight. How unfortunate." If a regular customer asks you to play a Beatles song but you don't do Beatles music, tell him or her you'll learn it and do it the next time you're at the club. Then do just that. If a goofy drunk comes up to the stage while you're on break and starts fooling with your microphone to address his pals, either tell him to buzz off or call the bartender or manager to remove him. But if a nasty drunk starts dissing you, just ignore him. He wants to get you into a confrontation, which would send the wrong message to the club owner.

BE PROFESSIONAL

Don't allow yourself to be bullied by impatient sound men, club owners, or emcees. Let nothing prevent you from doing the best show you can. If you break a string on stage, either stop the show and change it quickly off stage, or change it in front of the audience while you amuse them with a story. Don't try to struggle on with impaired equipment, unless you're about to end the show. And keep personal business personal. Above all, don't be late.

BECOME YOUR OWN BEST CRITIC

Be honest about what doesn't work with your show. Develop a healthy sense of yourself as a performer and a person. For the most part, don't expect truthful criticism from your friends or family—they would rather lie to you than hurt your feelings. If you're truly open to change and willing to learn from your mistakes, you will definitely have a smooth performance.

How to Find People to Play with

Susan Streitwieser

You've been playing guitar for a while now, you've developed a technique and style that works for you, your confidence is high, and you just need one thing before you hit that jam session, stage, or studio: other musicians! Finding musicians to play with is like finding a combination of the perfect job and the perfect mate. It's hard enough to find someone you get along with, but to find someone who also shares your artistic taste, your vision, your dedication, and your schedule can be a daunting task. Luckily, the world is packed with musicians who are looking for *you.* If you put enough energy and thought into your search, it's just a matter of time until you find your musical mate(s). Here are some steps that can help.

GET PREPARED

What are you going to say to the bass player you meet at Borders who asks you what you do? Can you describe the music you like and what your abilities are in an easy sound bite? "I'm a great lead player, and I want to put together an acoustic Nirvana cover band." Keep it simple. The bassist may not be right for you, but a friend of hers might be, so you want something easy to remember. No one likes to pigeonhole himself (we're all originals, aren't we?), but try to put yourself in a ballpark.

What do you want? Another guitarist at your level with whom you can jam? A band that is dedicated to getting a record deal? A once-a-week casual jazz gig at the corner coffeehouse? Get very clear about your goals. The clearer you are, the smaller the chance that you'll be sidetracked by musicians who aren't right for you.

What can you offer? Musicians will play with you for a variety of reasons. It's pretty easy to lure musicians to a jam session (many are known to follow the scent of free beer and chips), but securing the level of commitment required for starting and maintaining a band is quite another matter. Some players have a no pay, no play rule. For a struggling artist barely able to scrape together pick money, this may be a deal breaker. But paying your musicians does have a definite advantage: you get to be in charge. "She who signs the checks calls the tunes." If you want musicians to play for free, however, you may need to offer them something else. If you write all the songs, are you willing to split future royalties with the band? Do you have a lead on a paying gig? Great contacts? Don't be discouraged if all you have is talent, vision, and drive—a dream and a well-thought-out plan can be very seductive. And be honest. I have voice students who have hooked up with musicians by saying something like, "I have no track record, I've never performed, but I've studied voice for two years and my teacher says I'm great."

Susan's Room: Susan Streitwieser and Tom Manche.

Where will you compromise? Your dream band can readily be found . . . in your dreams. The real world usually offers up something less. Will you join a band that loves your playing but refuses to play your songs? What if you find the perfect band, but they want you to be the bassist? What if that great singer can only rehearse Sundays from three to four o'clock? You want to be flexible without getting stuck in a situation that's worlds away from your goal. Know ahead of time what your limits are.

GET ORGANIZED

The first words spoken when two musicians get together to play are, "So what do you know, dude?" Make a list of the songs you play. If you play from sheet music or chord charts, gather them into a folder. (If you use a capo on some songs, it wouldn't hurt to transpose your charts to the right key.) Make copies. If you're doing original music, make a tape of it. Many musicians will want to hear your songs before agreeing to play with you, and it's easier to carry around a tape than a guitar. Don't spend too much money on this pre-demo tape; a solo guitar or guitar/vocal tape will get your songs across sufficiently. If your songs aren't finished, get your lyric scraps together in a notebook. If you have the money and determination, another avenue is to record a more elaborate demo that more clearly shows your musical vision and abilities. It'll give you something splashier with which to market yourself when you meet prospective musical partners and producers. The world is filled with producer/engineers who have their own studios, and they usually have a stable of musicians they use on their projects. Lastly, make a list of any relevant contacts you have: photographers, booking agents, graphic artists, etc.

GET THE WORD OUT

Tell everyone you know that you're looking for a band. Everyone has a musician cousin, neighbor, friend, or employee.

Throw a party or jam session. Invite every musician you know and tell them to bring every musician they know. If you are new to jam sessions, it wouldn't hurt to hire an experienced player (preferably a local name musician) to keep the ball rolling. Plus you'll attract more players if you can say, "Yeah, and Joe Blow the Killer Bassist will be there." You don't have to limit your networking to music parties, either. My husband and I have a monthly salon where we invite people to discuss political and social issues. When we needed a bass player for our band, we realized that we could choose from three bassists who were regular salon attendees!

Use the classified ads in a local music magazine. It's tough dealing with strangers, and you may meet with some attitude, but there are some great musicians out there using ads. Treat these as you would personal ads: don't give out your address; check each other out on the phone. Consider placing your own ad. Read other classifieds to get an idea of what to include. You want to describe yourself and your goals with a minimum of words. For example, "Intermediate acoustic guitarist into Natalie Merchant and Grateful Dead seeks musicians/singers to jam with for fun only." "Pro flatpicker wants to join deal-minded bluegrass band. Dedication a must." Musician-wanted ads are found in free local weeklies more often than in major daily newspapers (musicians are not the most affluent of people). Look for alternative weeklies in coffee shops and libraries. Also look in guitar and music stores for periodicals geared toward local musicians. Don't bother with ads in national magazines unless you're a member of a well-funded touring band.

Read bulletin boards. These can be hard to find in larger cities (like Los Angeles, where I live). They're especially valuable for finding musicians in your neighborhood. Look in instrument and sheet music stores, but also check out boards at your local coffee shop or grocery store.

Check the Internet. It is chock-full of bulletin boards and resources. Look for newsgroups, bulletin boards, and Web sites for your region to narrow your search. You can also use your style of music with a search engine, but you could be overwhelmed by the results. I used "finding acoustic guitarists" with the AOL search engine, and 600,000 documents were found! So many Web sites are linked to other Web sites now that you could probably start at any of the following: Web sites for your local music paper, music store, favorite club or coffeehouse, or local band.

Sign up with musician contact services. They cost money, but they can have listings you won't find elsewhere. You'll find ads for them in the back of music-oriented periodicals.

SETTING UP AN OPEN MIC

Q *How do I go about starting an open-mic night? What kind of equipment do I need?*

A Setting up an open mic shouldn't be too difficult; finding a venue is often the hardest part. Depending on the size of the place and the crowd, you might find that you can get away without any PA equipment, making it more an open stage than an open mic. There's a café close to where I live in San Francisco that does it that way, and it works out really well.

If you feel that you need a PA, you have a lot of choices. Probably the simplest thing to do would be to get a package deal that includes two speakers and a combined amplifier/mixer. Companies like Carvin, Crate, Fender, and JBL all offer basic systems like this, with prices starting at around $500. It's always a good idea to get the speakers off the floor on stands. You'll also need a couple of mics (sturdy ones like Shure SM57s or SM58s are a good choice), mic stands, and cables to hook everything up. Having a DI box would also be nice, as it improves the sound of pickups plugged directly into the mixer. You should familiarize yourself with the equipment before using it live for the first time to avoid problems.

Once you have a place and whatever equipment you think you need, it's time to do some advertising. At the very least, put up some flyers in the venue itself a few weeks ahead of time. If you're in a small town, you can probably get the local papers to write an announcement about the event. Talk it up among all the musicians you know; the more people that show up the first time, the better. Think about how you want to structure the evening. How will you decide the order of the performers? How much time will each performer get? What does it take to be a good emcee?

I find that the best open mics are the ones that take place regularly at a set time (such as every other Friday night). That way people don't have to call ahead to find out whether it's on, and it's easier to build a regular crowd.

—*Teja Gerken*

GET OUT INTO THE WORLD

It's time-consuming but fun, and it can be the best way to meet people. Go to clubs and coffeehouses, preferably ones that play your style of music. When you find one you like, try to go fairly often, even if a band you don't know is playing. You'll feel more at home and be braver about meeting people when you're a regular. If you like a band or artist, approach them (but not when they are hurriedly clearing their stuff from the stage). Most musicians appreciate the attention, and you never know if they might be looking for new players.

Go to open mics. Go whether you perform or not. Lots of solo artists are looking to be more than solo. I've found most people at Los Angeles open mics to be very friendly, and I've also seen performers at open mics say things like, "I just met this guy out back and he's going to sit in on this next song." If you're looking for singers, you'll find loads of them at piano bars. If you are past the beginner stage, some clubs have full bands with which you can sit in: look for jam night listings in the paper. Some of these sessions are open; some are invitation only. Often you can wrangle an invitation if you go and hang

RESOURCES FOR FINDING MUSICIANS

PERFORMING-RIGHTS ORGANIZATIONS

ASCAP. Los Angeles (323) 883-1000, New York (212) 621-6000, Nashville (615) 742-5000; www.ascap.com.

BMI. Los Angeles (310) 659-9109, New York (212) 586-2000, Nashville (615) 401-2000; www.bmi.com.

SESAC. New York (212) 586-3450, Nashville (615) 320-0055; www.sesac.com.

GATHERINGS

California Coast Music Camp. (650) 306-0399; www.infopoint.com/orgs/ccmc.

Kerrville Folk Festival. (830) 257-3600; www.kerrville-music.com.

Folk Alliance. (202) 835-3655; www.folk.org. Hosts an annual conference and regional meetings and also publishes the *North American Folk Business Directory*, which lists acoustic musicians, clubs, coffeehouses, organizations, festivals, radio stations, periodicals, and more.

Puget Sound Guitar Workshop. (360) 647-2979; www.psgw.org.

Swannanoa Gathering. (828) 298-3325, ext. 426; www.swangathering.org.

out several times. Open mics change continually, so check your local weekly for club and coffeehouse listings.

Professional organizations like ASCAP, BMI, SESAC (all performing rights societies), and NAS (National Academy of Songwriters) often have industry showcases and classes that are loaded with other musicians. While many of them take place in Los Angeles, Nashville, or New York, they also run or sponsor regional events in San Francisco, Seattle, Chicago, Chapel Hill, and elsewhere. Check into songwriter and music organizations for your area as well.

Go to music festivals. Festival campgrounds are crammed with soon-to-jam or jamming musicians. Use common sense and good manners about joining an ongoing jam session, but in general you'll find loads of friendly players. Many musicians go to the Kerrville Folk Festival in Texas simply to hang out with fellow musicians and end up skipping the scheduled concerts! Not all festivals are conducive to campground jamming, however. I camped at the Telluride Bluegrass Festival one freezing June, and people disappeared into tents at night and thawed out by day watching the performers. Staffers will know if their festival is jam-friendly. Call ahead.

Attend guitar camps and music classes. Guitar and music camps are incredibly fun, and they're a great place to find musicians. If you're shy about playing with other musicians, this is the place to start; guitar camp staffers and teachers are notorious for their ability to painlessly ease you into jam sessions. If you're more advanced, you'll find loads of like-minded players who would like nothing more than to jam until sunrise. The camps are filled with smart, funny, working adults like you. Go to one even if you *aren't* looking for musicians; you'll have a blast.

I've taken several classes where the people I met were the highlight of the class. You'll have better luck finding someone playing at your level in a guitar technique class, but you'll also find musicians in theory, songwriting, and music business classes. Your local music store and/or community college may offer classes, and class listings can also be found in the back of your local weekly. If you're feeling brave, you can even call private music teachers to ask if they have any students playing at your level who are looking for musicians to play with.

One of the best things about going out is that you'll meet and befriend other musicians. They may not all share your exact musical goals or abilities, but there's nothing like being part of a community of musicians to keep you happy and on track throughout your musical search and beyond.

A final inspirational story: When I moved to L.A. I knew exactly three people in town. I immediately sent my demo tape to the local music paper's demo review columnist, then spent my first eight months going to every open mic and club I could find. (By the way, you'll meet more people if you go by yourself.) I met my bass player at an open mic and my coproducer at a club. My demo was finally reviewed the following summer, and I subsequently received a call from a producer/engineer/guitarist who'd read the review and liked my material enough to offer me spec studio time to record my first album. While recording the album, we formed a band and then got married! So get motivated, get organized, and get out there!

Busking

Judith Antonelli

One-man band Eric Royer regales Cambridge pedestrians with his solo bluegrass act.

It's rush hour at Park Street station, the center of Boston's subway system. The weather is hot and muggy, and the shoulder-to-shoulder crowd is sweaty and tired-looking after another day's work. All of a sudden there is the blast of some loud, obnoxious music. Looking around, I see what seems to be just another guy with a boom box. But then the guy pulls out a flute and starts playing, using the boom box as his backup band. The music is completely transformed; it sounds terrific! The crowd perks up, a few people drop money into his open flute case, and here in this grungy underground tunnel, the revitalizing power of music once again becomes evident.

Who are these modern urban minstrels, these subway and street musicians who entertain the city's commuters for spare change? The answers are varied and often quite surprising. They range from amateur to professional musicians, from full-fledged bands with fancy amplification equipment to a guy who just claps his hands and sings a cappella, and from people who make small change to a guy who pulls in as much as $200 a day.

Gonzalo Silva, a singer-songwriter who plays bass guitar, makes his living—"equivalent to a good part-time job," he says—playing on the street and in subway stations. With drummer Jason Gardner, Silva plays for three to four hours a day, five days a week. His average income, he says, is $12 an hour. "Street playing fuels my desire to become a full-time musician and is a way to advance my career," he explains during a break at the Brattle Street station in Harvard Square. "Playing in urban downtown areas gives you courage. I've also explored the New York scene. The attitude there is tolerant; in Boston it's appreciative. The difference, if you're not confident, can really work against you."

At the other end of the spectrum is self-taught guitarist Sergei Alexeev, who has a nine-to-five job and plays in subway stations in his spare time. The money is secondary. "I'm not a subway musician," he says. "I'm just practicing. I can't do this at home or my neighbors will call the cops. This is a great place to practice." Alexeev plays a custom-made electric guitar, uses a keyboard to produce prerecorded music (he presses one key and it keeps playing), and is surrounded by a bunch of little boxes that provide sound effects.

Bobby Wilson, a housepainter by trade, plays his acoustic guitar in the Park Street and Quincy subway stations with no amplification whatsoever. "I don't need it," he says simply, after crooning "My Cherie Amour." Playing a genre of music he calls "any broken love song," Wilson performs up to six hours at a time at least twice a week and earns $10 to $15 an hour. "Sometimes the people are the entertainment," he notes. "The people who want to listen the least usually stand right in front of me. One woman complained to me that she couldn't hear the announcements [over the subway station loudspeakers], and 25 people said to her, 'What do you *want* to hear them for?'"

Generally speaking, to be either a street or a subway musician requires a permit. Different cities have different rules, but to play, for example, in Cambridge, Massachusetts—most musicians choose Harvard Square—you have to pay $40 a year to the Cambridge Arts Council and follow the regulations about decibel level, hours, and location. No musician can play within 50 feet of another musician; within 100 feet of a school, church, or library that's open; or in front of a hospital at any time. To play in the Boston subway system, you have to go to the MBTA (Massachusetts Bay Transit Authority) office in person. The permit is free, it's good for three months, and you can play at any hour (the subways stop running at 12:45 A.M.) and at any location. The permit only stipulates "no drugs" and "no drums."

But even if you can't play your drums in the subway tunnel, you *can* pound on buckets, pots, and refrigerator parts! That's what full-time subway musician Geronimo Gaspar does. He makes his own music on three institutional-size plastic buckets placed upside-down on metal refrigerator racks, two porcelain refrigerator bins (the kind you keep your vegetables in) turned on their sides, and a couple of upside-down aluminum pots. He schlepps all of this around by subway in one of those collapsible upright shopping carts. It's unbelievable how great he sounds. What's even more unbelievable is his income—he says he makes $70 to $200 a day, playing ten hours at a time.

During the summer, when tourists flock to Boston, Faneuil Hall and Quincy Market provide other locations for musicians of every stripe. Gerry Mack plays blues, jazz, and R&B on an electric keyboard two or three times a week, but he doesn't do it for the fun of it. "As a blind person, I couldn't get and keep a straight job," he explains, pointing out that the unemployment rate for people with disabilities is 70 percent. "I would prefer other options, but it beats the hell out of not working."

Lawrence Sullivan, a teenager who's by far the youngest street musician around town and has been performing since the age of three, is a musical whiz. He plays drums, piano, saxophone, harmonica, and guitar, and also acts, tap-dances, and performs as a ventriloquist. When I catch his act in Harvard Square, he "only" has his drums, keyboard, and sax with him, and his father hovers protectively nearby. Although he has performed at clubs, toured U.S. and European jazz festivals, and appeared on TV, Sullivan says he enjoys playing on the street.

Gonzalo Silva (left) and Jason Gardner play Boston's Brattle Street station.

It's not just amateur musicians with no other alternative who play the subway station/street corner circuit. Professional musicians do it for a kind of exposure they say is unique. For example, Nazca—the name of a band as well as the pre-Incan Peruvian culture from which its four members originate—can be found playing Andean music in Harvard Square about three times a month. Even though they have traveled the world (New York, Miami, Spain, France, Japan) playing concerts, festivals, and private parties, they still like to play on the street. "That's how we get our [paying] jobs," says Daniel Castro, one of the band's two wind-instrument players. The other, Ryan Bazan, adds, "We are trying to make Andean music popular around the world." On a good day, he says, they sell 20 to 25 CDs and cassettes.

Another professional group that still likes to play on the streets of Boston is Division St. Although this four-man rock 'n' roll band has released two CDs, plays clubs, and has even done some high-profile concerts (opening for Jewel and Sarah McLachlan), the band can be found in front of Faneuil Hall on a regular basis. "It's a very open forum," says acoustic guitarist and lead singer Isaac Hasson. "There are so many people. We catch them off guard and it's very unpredictable." The band's manager, David Oriola, adds, "We reach a lot more people here than by playing inside. It's like going on the road, only the road comes to you instead." Oriola "discovered" the band three years ago while they were playing at the Downtown Crossing subway station. Since then, they have sold 12,000 CDs.

So if you're ready to play out but not ready for the club or café scene, consider your local subway station (or bus stop or public square). You never know when you'll be spotted by a music-industry professional lurking in the crowd, waiting for a train home.

Bookstore Gigs

Teja Gerken

Acoustic venues are scarce nowadays, and the recent boom of bookstore chains such as Borders and Barnes and Noble means hundreds of new performance opportunities across the country. Most of these stores present a mixture of local talent and well-known acts promoting their new CDs, and one look at the bookstores' performance calendars confirms a soft spot for acoustic music. Playing these gigs is a great way to learn how to promote yourself, work with a (usually basic) PA, structure a set, and just get some experience performing in front of strangers. If you're already a seasoned performer, the bookstore gig can help you tap into a new audience, sell your CD (although you have to clear this with the store manager in advance), work on new material, and—especially if you're on the road—make a little money between bigger gigs.

LINING UP THE GIG

The best way to get started is to go to a scheduled performance at a store where you're interested in playing—ideally a performance that's stylistically similar to your own. Talk to the musician and ask how he or she liked the gig. More importantly, find out the name and direct phone number of the store's events coordinator. Later, when you call the person who does the booking, explain what type of music you play and ask if he or she would like you to send a demo. A typical demo pack includes a tape or CD (a good home recording should do the trick), a picture (preferably a black-and-white eight-by-ten), and a short bio. The more professional this package looks, the better. You should also find out how much performers are paid. Sometimes you can choose between a check and a store credit, and the latter usually amounts to more. If the store is part of a national chain, don't assume that the pay is the same at every location. Also find out if a PA will be provided and whether there are any other requirements you should know about.

Wait a couple of weeks before you make a follow-up call; most bookstore event coordinators wear many hats, and it might take them a while to get to your demo. Hopefully your phone will ring within a reasonable amount of time and you'll be offered a time slot, usually about six to eight weeks in the future. Congratulations!

PLANNING YOUR SHOW

Now it's time to do a little planning for the actual gig. Most likely you'll be expected to play two one-hour sets. When you choose the songs you're going to play, keep in mind that there will be other stuff going on during your performance. People will be browsing, reading, talking, studying. It's not the ideal set of circumstances to show the world what a great player you are, but there is usually a core group of listeners who are genuinely interested in the music. Stay away from material that creates too much of a ruckus, is potentially offensive, or is so difficult that nobody understands it. Think about some things to say about the pieces. Remember that most of your audience will be there by chance and will therefore know nothing about you.

GEAR

Think about what equipment you want to bring. Generally, the simpler the setup, the better. Nobody wants to hear you do a two-hour sound check. There won't be anyone there to help you run the PA, so you should be familiar with its basic functions. You might want to bring your own mic and mic stand. I highly recommend using a guitar with a pickup. Imagine the squeal of a hot microphone in the midst of those quiet shoppers and coffee sippers! A pickup will also make it easier to control your volume, which should be high on your list of priorities.

TIME TO PLAY

Plan to arrive at the store an hour or so before you're scheduled to start playing. See if the person who booked you is there. If not, ask if there is anyone else who can show you where to set up. If there is a café in the store, that's most likely where you'll be playing, but you might have the option of playing in another part of the store. Once you're done with your setup and sound check, take a few minutes to relax. Get a latté if there's a café (usually free for performers) and get a feel for the place and its people. You'll probably have to ask a staff member to turn off the canned music, and if it's a big store, ask if they can introduce you over the intercom. As with any performance, start out with one of your stronger songs, and voilà, you're off! Welcome to the world of bookstore gigs.

How to Succeed as an Opening Act

Cosy Sheridan

Being the opening act at someone else's show can be the best gig in the world or the worst. In the best of all possible worlds, you play 25 minutes of your best material, sell lots of CDs to new fans, and come back to play your own show in six months. In the worst case, you play to people who wish you weren't there and make no bones about letting you know.

Let's start with the basics. Question: Why do you want to be an opening act? Answer: For exposure (which, my first music guru, Harvey Reid, always reminded me, is "a leading cause of death among Eskimos"). Exposure to whom? To the headliner's audience? To the promoter? To the headliner?

Your answer to that question should not be "to the headliner." Don't take the gig if all you want is a private audition with the headliner. It's not their job to listen to you. They have an entire concert to get geared up for that night, and it's nice of them just to lend you their audience. With some gracious and delightful exceptions, the people I've opened for have rarely come out of the dressing room until I was done.

Singer-songwriter Catie Curtis recently toured with Mary Chapin Carpenter as the opener. She said Carpenter was "very supportive, not only by inviting me on the tour, but by mentioning me in her set and inviting me out to sing at the end." Curtis has also toured as an opening act for an electric blues performer, and she says that it's best to open for someone whose music is as similar to your own as possible.

Instrumental guitarist Ken Bonfield offers a different take. He says he would rather open for a singer-songwriter than another instrumentalist. "For the audience," he says, "that can be just too many notes in a night."

Many promoters go by the general rule that men should open for women, and women should open for men. I have opened for women and it has worked just fine, and I have opened for men where it didn't work at all. I think this rule relies too much on the mistaken idea that all women sound alike and all men sound alike.

GETTING THE GIG

Each club or coffeehouse has its own way of lining up opening acts. At some coffeehouses, there is one person in charge of booking the headliner and someone else who books the openers. At other clubs, the same person does both. Find out who you need to talk to and call them. Often you'll be leaving messages on their home answering machines or with their 11-year-old children, who may nor may not actually write down the message or get your phone number right. Don't be discouraged. Keep calling back.

Sometimes you'll get the opening gig through the headliner. It might be a friend or someone who just wants to help you out. Be sure to call the promoter and check with him or her; the headliner might have forgotten to mention that they invited you to perform. Ask the promoter if he or she would like you to send a picture and/or some promotional material. Also find out what time you should be there for sound check.

Acoustic troubadour Cosy Sheridan.

KNOW YOUR AUDIENCE

An appropriate headliner will have an audience demographic that is similar to yours. For instance, I recently had a fine, male singer-songwriter open for me. He looked out the door of the green room at my audience, which tends to be made up of 35- to 50-year-olds, and said to me with some trepidation, “Is this your standard audience?” “Yup,” I answered. He had recently been opening for Ellis Paul, whose audience is predominantly 18- to 30-year-olds, and he thought my audience demographic would be similar. He did just fine with my audience, but the point is that he knew who his audience was. Find out who your audience is. Are they mostly men or mostly women? Do they come from one age group or many? Are they urban? Are they married or single?

THE FINANCES

As the opening act, you're not getting a percentage of the tickets sold at the door. The standard amount is anywhere from $25 to $100. Obviously you're not going to pay your rent with this. The best way to make money as an opening act is to sell tapes or CDs. Most venues will let you set up a table in the lobby and sell them yourself. Some clubs will even do it for you. I have had some of my best-selling nights when I was the opening act.

Don't count on being allowed to put people on the guest list. At some level, you yourself are a guest. Remember that your guests are money out of the headliner's pocket. But it can't hurt to ask. Most of the time, it's OK for the opening act to invite one or two guests.

WATCH THE CLOCK

There are three rules to being an opening act: don't go over your time, don't go over your time, and don't go over your time. If the promoter tells you 20 minutes, that's what he or she means. It's a mark of a professional to keep to your time limit. I once opened for Janis

Ian at the Freight and Salvage in Berkeley. The first thing I said to the audience was, "Hi, I'm your opening act, and I'd like to assure you that I'm wearing a watch."

When putting together your set, figure four to five minutes for each song, including the introductory stage patter. Time yourself at other gigs to be sure. Remember that you'll spend time putting on your capo or retuning your guitar. Have a concise introduction worked out for each tune. If you get to the end of your third song and there are only four minutes left in your 20-minute time allotment, say "Thank you very much" and get off the stage early. When in doubt, go short. It leaves a good impression, and you might just get an encore if you leave a little bit of extra time.

THE GREEN ROOM

In many small clubs, there will only be one green room. As the opener, you may or may not get access to that green room. I have warmed up in many lobbies, singing quietly into the corner near the pay phone. If you do have access to the green room, remember that it is for warming up and for privacy. Unless you're the headliner, don't invite anyone back stage to visit.

SOUND CHECK

The general rule on sound checks is that they're done in reverse order as the show: the last performer checks first, the first performer checks last. The headliner's sound check may run right up to the time they open the door, so be prepared for the possibility that you'll have to do your sound check as people are being seated. Know what sort of sound you like and how to ask for it. For instance, I tell the sound engineer, "I don't need a direct box. I have a Fishman Blender. All I need is a low-impedance mic cord. I like a sort of bassy guitar sound, with the guitar and voice level pretty equal in the mix, and I like reverb." This gives him or her an idea of where to go.

Keep yourself portable. Picks, capos, tuner, extra strings, cords—have them all in a bag, easily and quickly accessible. Lots of effects boxes and foot pedals are going to slow you down. Practice changing a string quickly and bring a string winder and clippers to the gig.

LIGHTEN UP

It's possible that your first song will be your sound check. Relax and let the audience know what is going on. Keep it lighthearted: "Hey, you don't know what I sound like anyhow."

Finally, be yourself. The audience doesn't expect you to be a seasoned performer. And in most instances, they're rooting for you to succeed.

Playing in Restaurants

Gary Joyner

John Lehmann-Haupt serenades diners at Windows on the World.

You've spent a lot of time and energy developing the craft of guitar playing. You've done some coffeehouse gigs for 25 bucks and a pound of beans. Now you want to be paid fairly for your hard-won skills. Many players seek work in restaurants, where the small, portable guitar can provide full-voiced, pianistic instrumental music. Busy Seattle performer John Miller calls restaurant gigging "blue-collar musician work that has been done for as long as there have been musicians." It's steady work, and if you play your cards right, it pays decent money. Let's take a look at the keys to being a successful restaurant musician and gather some advice from six guitarists who've put in a lot of time playing music among the white tablecloths and clinking glasses.

GETTING THE GIG

Agents don't book restaurants because there simply isn't enough money in it for them. You have to line up this kind of work for yourself. Musicians provide a service to restaurants, setting the tone for a pleasant dining experience. Your first task is to communicate the fact that you can provide this service in a professional manner. Return calls when you say you will. Show up early for meetings. Approach establishments that offer live

Musical restaurant workers: John Miller and John Reischman.

music to see if they have any openings. Approach ones that don't yet have live music and apply amiable persuasion to convince the manager that live music will improve business. Mid-afternoon is the best time to make contact, after the lunch rush and before dinner preparations get into full swing.

A little promotional material can be useful. A simple, down-to earth format will be most effective. A business card, a demo tape, and maybe a brief resumé or brochure are all you need. John Miller minimizes the value of promotional material. "You run a better chance if you can audition for them instead of dropping off a tape," he explains. "They simply want to know if you will make the dining experience better for their patrons." If you do use a tape, it should show as much variety as possible in less than four minutes. People make up their minds quickly, so full-length pieces will not be effective. Fade each tune on the tape after 30–45 seconds with a three-second count between tunes.

Concord Vista recording artist Jeff Linsky, well known for his masterful solo playing on a nylon-string requinto, found his first restaurant work in Hawaii with a repertoire of seven tunes. He identifies self-confidence as a primary asset in his career, as important as his remarkable ability to improvise. Linsky quotes Gene Leis, a music business entrepreneur and personal mentor: "'Everyone wants to feed a fat hog.' If people believe you are in demand, they want you. Remember, most people can't tell the difference between a great player and a student player. Mostly it's about being able to meet the needs of the situation, to play the music that people will enjoy and recognize."

Develop a mailing list to let people know when you play at a restaurant. The owners will love the extra business you bring. Keep a sign-up sheet beside a stack of business cards at gigs. This can lead to casuals, the one-night private parties and corporate gigs that pay three to five times more than restaurant work.

Your list of contacts will quickly become too big to manage in your head. A system for keeping records becomes mandatory. Buy a loose-leaf notebook and set aside one page for each prospect. Include the company name, contact person, phone numbers and addresses, the musical needs of the establishment, notes from conversations, and dates that you talked or left a tape.

John Lehmann-Haupt is a veteran guitarist in New York City who played for 12 years at Windows on the World atop the World Trade Center. To stay organized, he uses a file system of three-by-five cards that he finds more convenient and accessible than computer programs. Each card carries basic contact information plus the details and date (including year!) of each conversation, and what he's done for the client. He also suggests that you never send material without calling first. "You might as well throw it in the waste basket and save the postage. Leaving messages on a machine is also weak. Get the person on the phone and communicate in 20 seconds what you propose to do for them. Send your tape and make a note in your calendar to call them again in two weeks."

Decide at the outset whether you are willing to offer free previews. Mike Wollenberg, who performs an average of five nights a week in the San Francisco Bay Area, says, "I view it as a business. Salespeople often give out free samples. It comes under promotional expenses." He leaves a tape and brochure and follows up a few days later. "If they haven't listened to the tape, I say, 'I know you're busy. Why don't you let me come in and play for an hour? You can see how it will work.'" Chris Grampp, another Bay Area restaurant regular, fell into a great three-year solo job after playing a free gig for fun at a restaurant with a Dixieland band.

Solo performer Gary Joyner.

Big-city hotels often have exclusive arrangements with contractors. Even then, making contact with a banquet maître d' or head waiter can provide private party gigs that pay well. Lehmann-Haupt offers this insider tip: "In a hotel that doesn't have a commitment with a contractor, contact the food and beverage manager. They are busy, but you can get them. Pitch them quickly and then send a tape and resumé."

GETTING PAID

The amount of money you can expect to charge a restaurant will vary from one region to another. It's common practice to have a minimum price for two hours of work with a lower fee for each additional hour. Tony Hauser, who plays three to four nights a week in Minneapolis, has developed the ability to gauge what a restaurant can afford to pay. He stops in to see how they are doing on the nights he wants to work, notices the neighborhood to get an idea of the kind of rent they're paying, counts their tables, and reads the menu for prices. "A real kicker is whether or not they have a liquor license," he says.

Many establishments will let you bolster your income with a tip bowl. Tips are unpredictable, so it's not good to depend on them in lieu of an acceptable fee. CD sales can also affect the financial viability of a restaurant gig. You might make more from CD sales than from your fee. Confirm management policies regarding tips and product sales ahead of time.

Contracts are rarely used. Restaurant gigs are often on a week-to-week basis, if not night-to-night. A firm business manner and a clear idea of what you are willing to put up with will serve you well.

CHOOSING REPERTOIRE

It can be unnerving to play for people who don't seem to be listening. "The whole point of playing in a restaurant," explains John Lehmann-Haupt, "the difference between being able to do it and not being able to do it, is understanding that there *is* communication, but it's subliminal. If you don't understand that, you are going to be frustrated and not able to hack it. Tone quality and phrasing are more important than absolute technical perfection. The noise masks the details but not the sonority and phrase shape."

Watch feet and hands to see if you are getting through to people. You'll see them unconsciously keeping time to the music as they chat and eat, a sure sign that the music is working. You will quickly get an idea of the music that is most effective.

Wireless guitarist Mike Wollenberg.

Tony Hauser carefully paces his repertoire for a private dinner party. "There's a rhythm you go through with a gig. While people mill around before dinner, I play familiar up-tempo music. In a dining situation, I play classical music. During dinner I watch for the main course, when diners will be most quiet. That's when I do recognizable classics like 'Recuerdos de la Alhambra.' Then when they are drinking their coffee I pick it up again."

Familiar melodies will go over best, so include a varied selection of well-known warhorses in your playlist. Pop and jazz standards from every era are effective, as well as folk, Brazilian, bossa nova, Latin, jazz, and even television themes or familiar commercial jingles. The most frequently requested pop songs are Beatles songs, so learn as many of them as you can. With the number of families dining out these days, children's tunes are in high demand as well. Look to *Sesame Street* and Disney films for material. Work up a couple of variations of "Happy Birthday": a simple accompaniment for group singing and an entertaining and novel instrumental version. Fake books can be clumsy to use, and they significantly add to the weight of material you need to haul. Classical players may require sheet music, but if you play pop music you are better off memorizing tunes.

Songs should not be longer than two or three minutes. You want to keep things lively and moving. Most restaurant players find that a few thematic variations are more suitable than extended improvisations. Lehmann-Haupt observes, "If you play pre-ordained arrangements, you actually are improvising, but in different areas—nuance, rhythm, phrasing, dynamics, and tone color. I never get tired of playing the same things night after night, because they are never identical."

HANDLING REQUESTS

The topic of requests is a thorny one. If someone requests a piece you know, by all means play it. But think carefully before you decide to solicit requests. A relatively small repertoire of 150 songs with good variety can create the feeling of a larger repertoire, but inviting requests will cause problems unless you're prepared to have a minimum repertoire of 500–1,000 songs. Be aware that people making requests can fall into a little game that abuses the situation and spoils the rhythm of your performance. Jeff Linsky and John Miller enjoy the challenge of playing a song that they've never played before, improvising an arrangement on the spot. This daunting skill begins to seem humanly possible when you realize that the great majority of pop songs are built on relatively few chord progressions. Don't expect to learn to do it overnight, though. Jerry Coker's book, *Hearin' the Changes: Dealing with Unknown Tunes by Ear* (Advance Music, available from Sher Music Co., PO Box 445, Petaluma, CA 94953) is a valuable resource if you want to pursue this facility.

Here's a way to control request situations. When you finish playing a request, go quickly into another song. If you pause, someone is likely to toss out another request and you'll run the risk of getting into a game of Stump the Performer. The same maneuver can apply if you get a round of spontaneous applause after a song. Applause can create discomfort for the audience and the performer. Should they applaud after the next song? Your best bet is to acknowledge the applause briefly and then play a couple of tunes without a break. The discomfort will pass, and you can resume your normal routine.

DEALING WITH STAFF

Tony Hauser matches the mood to the food.

You will soon become aware of your impact on the house staff—waiters, bussers, hosts, etc. Those folks are working very hard, and they deserve your respect. Chris Grampp points out, "They are like emergency-room staff. They don't have time to deal with anything but their customers." Be mindful of how your activities affect them. Look for areas of heavy traffic and keep your gear out of the way. Find the location of the jukebox switch and the coffeepot so you won't have to bother staff.

It is to your advantage if the staff sees you as a person who is also doing a job and not as some temperamental outsider who has come to get in their way. "You have to be part of the team," Mike Wollenberg explains. "In one place I could order off the menu, but the staff was served an employee meal. After a while they resented that fact. So I said, 'Why don't I just have the employee meal?' If they see you drinking wine, playing music, and getting paid, there could also be some resentment." And even when a meal is part of your pay, it's wise to leave a courtesy tip.

No matter how much material you have, the staff is going to get tired of it. Mike Wollenberg puts it this way, "I play as much to the staff of the restaurant as to the customers. When somebody who works there says, 'You ought to check out this song' or 'I love this song, do you think you can learn it?' even if I only halfway like the tune I will always try to learn it. You want to keep the staff on your side."

FINDING THE RIGHT GEAR

In all but the smallest rooms you will need amplification that can cut through restaurant noise with clarity. Portability is often the most important factor. Several of the performers I interviewed for this article couldn't immediately identify the brand of amp they used, but they could describe in detail the streamlined way they transported it. A small two-wheeler, especially one that converts into a cart, can be a lifesaver.

Any guitar that cuts through restaurant noise will work. Players use nylon-strings, steel-string flattops, and archtops successfully for solo gigs. Jeff Linsky uses a requinto, a three-quarter–size Spanish guitar, while Chris Grampp plays fingerstyle arrangements on a purple Stratocaster. John Lehmann-Haupt dislikes the sound of piezo pickups, so he mounts a microphone on the edge of his classical guitar with a small gooseneck. Tony Hauser's favorite traveling rig includes a Baggs pickup in his Ramírez guitar, which he runs through a battery-powered MaxiMouse amp. "For some weird reason, if it's not cranked to the max, the MaxiMouse and Baggs combination gets a surprisingly natural sound," he says. "Anything to avoid carrying a microphone and stand!"

Mike Wollenberg uses a unique wireless amplification method. The first transmitter carries his guitar signal to an amp. The second transmitter relays the signal to an input in the house stereo system. It can take a half hour to set up. "You can get by with just one wireless system if you can plug your amp directly into the house system," he says. "That's preferable because you have less potential for things to go wrong." The sound from tiny ceiling speakers common in house systems is acceptable and well worth the ability to be heard throughout the room. You don't have to be a strolling musician to appreciate the benefits of the wireless system. Going wireless saves you from getting stuck in a corner. You can place yourself in assorted spots where people can see that the music is live and not Memorex.

PREPARING FOR PITFALLS

People who have worked in bands might find the solo situation intimidating. You can't lay back and let someone else carry the performance for a moment. A restaurant gig can actually be a good way to make the transition to being a solo performer. Learn to pace yourself by alternating difficult tunes with easier ones.

When you deal with the public, you set yourself up as a target for the release of frustrations by strangers. Alcohol consumption has a way of exacerbating untoward behavior. Sometimes you'll wonder why someone who dislikes guitar music would take the table directly in front of you. Your restraint and tact will occasionally be called upon. Try not to take it personally.

Murphy's Law has a way of asserting itself at gigs. You can best thwart it by being prepared. Arrive in plenty of time to set up and dress appropriately. Bring spare AC and guitar cords, a fuse for your amp, batteries, and strings. You may accidentally cause feedback or pull a plug that makes a loud noise. The fish-eyed stares you get might make you feel suddenly isolated. Maintain your demeanor, swallow the embarrassment, apologize, and carry on.

Chris Grampp remembers a particularly embarrassing situation. "I was playing at the Santa Fe Bar and Grill in Berkeley. Ex-governor Jerry Brown came in for dinner and sat down by himself. Four men wearing suits and dark sunglasses followed him in and sat at a table right next to him. I had to move my Fender Deluxe Reverb amp. The reverb was mistakenly turned up all the way. I bumped the amp, which sent out a ricocheting sound like gun shots. The guys who I assumed were security guards all stood up and reached inside their jackets, and I thought, 'Oh my God, I'm going to get gunned down in the restaurant.' Luckily, everything went back to normal."

GO FOR IT

It is possible to be creative while providing a valuable service in restaurants. In addition to making music, your imagination allows you to satisfy diverse needs, think on your feet, function as a team player who contributes to the overall environment, and get paid for your unique skills. There's really nothing magical about "professional experience"; it's simply about getting out there and doing it. Do some planning and then hop into the fray. You will learn as you go. Use the ideas here to hone your own strategy. Have a good gig!

House Concerts

Cosy Sheridan

House concerts—where music lovers turn their living rooms into down-home performance venues—have been part of the acoustic music scene for years, but recently they've reached a kind of critical mass. Thanks in part to the Internet, which has helped presenters share information and promote their shows, these informal concerts occur in virtually every part of the country, and some musicians now do entire tours of only house concerts. The phenomenon has become visible enough that, amazingly enough, it hit the front page of the *New York Times* in November 1999.

As a performer used to playing in clubs, bars, and coffeehouses, I found my first encounter with a house concert a bit unnerving. I missed the microphone stand. It had always been a nice, safe boundary between me and the audience. In house concerts, there are for the most part no stages and no sound systems—ergo, there are no natural boundaries. In a standard concert situation, you *know* where to stand: on the stage, where the lights are, behind the microphone. You *know* there will be at least four feet (if not 15) between you and the front row. In a house concert, you might be faced with a jumble of people sitting on pillows at your feet. It takes a while to get used to standing in what feels like the middle of nowhere—maybe where the rubber plant used to be—and singing and playing.

The author makes herself at home.

You need to learn to define a space for yourself. Find a chair or a table where you can put a glass of water or a cup of coffee, your picks, capo, and set list. If you sit down when you play, find a chair *and* a table. Spend some time on "your stage" before the audience arrives—grounding yourself in your performance space is key. Make sure you're comfortable. If you're not, the audience will sense it, and the show will end up being more about your not being grounded than about the music.

Another difference in a house concert is the lighting. It's amazing how effectively lights can focus the attention and energy in a room. There might be only four people in a club, but if the lights are off where the audience is and on where you are, you can give a concert with a fantasy audience of 300. Your average American living room does not have stage lights. If possible, your host might turn off all the lights in the room except for the one near you, but it's still going to feel different than a real stage. You're going to be looking right into your audience's eyes.

If this makes you nervous (as it used to make me), then get to know your audience before you start the concert. Talk to some of them, if possible, or at least stand in the room and observe them. I once played a house concert where the hosts had told me that they preferred I didn't put the concert on my mailing list because they already had an audience of friends and acquaintances. So I stood around while everyone came in and kind of scanned the crowd. I noticed that they didn't look familiar to me—somehow they didn't look like my typical audience. It wasn't the clothes or the hairstyles or the age; it was something subtle. And they clearly knew each other. I asked the host, and he told me that they mostly knew each other from work: they made bomb simulations for the Department of Defense. I ended up having a great time with the bomb simulators, but the lesson was to get to know your audience beforehand. In many cases, these folks won't be fans on your mailing list; they will be your host's friends. This can be a real advantage. One, your material is new to them, which always makes for a wonderful concert. And two, an audience that already knows each other is more comfortable, more willing to relax and feel whatever emotion your music evokes.

The audience at a house concert comes to meet the artist, to see who you are. They aren't expecting well-rehearsed stage patter and a slick show. They want to get to know you. Bruce Rouse, who has run a very successful house concert in Austin for the past nine years, has found that "the more interaction between the performer and audience, the better." The sort of show that doesn't work so well, he said, is "the person who shows up with a pat show. No introductions, no comments. The performer that works best is the one who can really interact with the audience." So, if you find audience intimacy pure torture, then house concerts might not be for you.

Most house concerts will have a built-in audience, but some will not. Ask the host or hostess about listing the concert in a mailing or on your Web site. They may prefer that you don't include their name or address, opting for something like "house concert," with the town and a phone number instead. Many house concerts are reservation-only, which also gives the host or hostess a way to prescreen the audience. The Panzer house concert series in Columbia, Maryland, requires reservations mostly because the house is always full, but also, said Sherry Panzer, so that "if somebody weird calls, we can say, 'Sorry, we're booked.'" This is a good safety measure.

If you're a touring musician, house concerts can be a great way to make friends and also can offer a night in a real home instead of a hotel. Ask your host if the policy includes housing the musicians.

One big difference between a club or concert venue and a house concert is the finances. The overhead is usually very low, so you can take home a sizable percentage (if not all) of the door. An established house concert series might already have a policy regarding whether or not to take expenses out of the pot. Some house concerts are supported by the finances of the host. The host pays for all of the phone calls and the food and mailing expenses. Some hosts take the expenses out of the money from the door and give the performer the rest. Ask your host about his or her policy beforehand. If it's a new venue for house concerts, or maybe if it's a friend hosting it for you, they might not be sure about what approach to take. Ask if they had any expenses and, if possible, offer to cover those expenses out of the door earnings.

There are lots of established house concerts around the country, but that doesn't mean those are the only ones you can play. People often have to drive a long way to a concert in a big city because there's no venue in their little town. If a fan tells you that he wishes there were somewhere for you to play in his town, tell him there is: his living room.

Of course, there are many other considerations and questions for the host of a house concert. How do you spread the word? How should you set up the room? What expenses should be passed on to the performer? Where will concertgoers park their cars? There are more and more resources for the would-be house concert host. Check out www.houseconcerts.com on the Web; the site is run by presenters in Texas but includes information on concert series in many other states.

House concerts are fun. Once you've become accustomed to their particular ins and outs, you'll find them to be some of the best venues to play.

Being a Side Musician

Scott Nygaard

Scott Nygaard jams with Tim O'Brien, Mark Schatz, and Jerry Douglas at the Telluride Bluegrass Festival.

There are many ways to be a performer. We don't all have the flamboyance and charisma to command center stage as star of a band or the chutzpah to sit alone on stage with only a guitar to entertain an audience. Being a member of a band is an obvious solution, but some people tire quickly of playing the same repertoire over and over or are not cut out for the subtle negotiations and compromises that being a member of a band entails. Some find that the spontaneity and excitement of being a freelance side musician, playing with a variety of performers with little rehearsal time, suit their temperament and abilities. For instance, one thing that I discovered a few years after Guitar-Playing Obsession Syndrome set in was that I wasn't very good at playing specific arrangements on stage. So I became an improviser by necessity—I had to do something when my mind went blank and my fingers forgot their way home. And since I had spent a lot of time as a teenager lying on my bed playing guitar along with the radio, I discovered that I was pretty good at improvising simple accompaniment licks (otherwise known as organized noodling) to a variety of songs. I soon discovered the joys of being a sideman.

BAND MEMBER OR FREELANCER?

There are two different ways to be a side musician. The most obvious is to simply become a member of someone's band. This has many advantages, from regular employment to not having to worry about much other than showing up to the gig on time—no promotion, no booking, etc. If you are lucky enough to hook up with a performer you love, this can be a great gig. The disadvantage of playing the same music night after night is outweighed by knowing that the music you make will be satisfying. Your repertoire may change regularly too—some performers are not shy about pulling out any song from their history and expecting you to follow right along in front of hundreds of people.

The other way to be a side musician is to freelance, taking gigs with a variety of performers in as many styles as you can manage. The advantage of this is that it keeps you on your musical toes. Depending on how many people you play with, you may have to be familiar with hundreds of songs, or have the ability to improvise and play songs you've never heard before at the drop of a hat. This is a great way to keep your playing from getting stale. The disadvantage is the disadvantage of most freelance work—no steady income. The number of your gigs will be up to the whims and vagaries of various performers' schedules and inclinations.

Some of the secrets to being a successful side musician are the same for both situations. The keys to being a good accompanist are having good ears, being flexible, and being able to react to what's happening without getting flustered. The ability to fluidly play songs you've never played before on stage is one of those things that looks like magic to outsiders. But with preparation, a good grounding in the clichés of your favorite style, an easygoing, ready-for-anything attitude, and the ability to concentrate intensely for short periods of time, you'll soon learn to pull the rabbit out of the hat.

DECIDE ON A STYLE

While many people enjoy playing different styles of music, it makes sense to concentrate on one or two styles if you want to be a side musician. Become as familiar as possible with the conventions of your chosen style. For instance, bluegrass bands and some blues singers think nothing of adding a measure or two while waiting for the singer to start the next verse, whereas swing and jazz bands would be horrified by any corruption of their standard 32- and 12-bar formats. And singer-songwriters will construct their songs out of any number of measures they wish. Learn the cues that signal what is coming next—these will differ somewhat from style to style. The more you can anticipate arrangements and follow accidental deviations from the standard arrangement, the more valuable you'll become. Take cues from the vocal, changes in the guitar harmony, and the bass line—all things that can signal the beginning of the next section or the ending. Spend lots of time at jam sessions and play along with records.

PREPARATION

The two ways most people get gigs as side musicians are by audition or by trial gig. If you're starting out, you'll either have to scan the musician want ads for auditions or hang out at jam sessions and hope that someone notices your brilliant playing. Trial gigs—when you sit in at a real show rather than in rehearsal—will really only happen once you've been playing on stage for awhile. Whether you're going to your first audition or you're a seasoned side musician, the more you prepare the better, even if you're an excellent off-the-cuff improviser. Good preparation will show the person you're auditioning for that you're serious about getting the gig. If a performer has recordings, get them and learn the material. Don't rely on the performer to send them to you. If they're commercially available (and with the Web, you can find anything), buy them yourself. If the performer doesn't have a CD, ask if he or she has a live tape. This is a good idea even when performers do have recordings, as their CDs may sound nothing like their live shows.

Make simple charts of all the songs you're likely to play. This is a good way to get an idea of the structure of the songs, as well as any unusual progressions, without actually memorizing them. I usually write down simple chord charts for the verse, chorus, bridge, and any variations of these using the Nashville number system—1 for the I chord, 4 for the IV chord, 2- for the II minor chord, and so on. Then I write out the structure of the song. For example: intro (half verse), verse, verse, chorus, instrumental break (whole verse), bridge, verse, chorus, chorus, ending (last line of chorus). Sometimes charts can be very simple. For instance, the song may just be a 12-bar blues played through a certain number of times with a four-bar vamp between each verse. Even if it seems simple enough to remember, write it down anyway. The very existence of these charts will impress the performer at an audition, and you can also review them backstage if you've got a trial gig with no rehearsal.

ETIQUETTE

The political or personal aspects of being a side musician are just as important as the musical. The important thing to remember at all times is that it is not your gig. You may get your fair share of glory, but the person whose name is on the marquee is going to bear the consequences when things go wrong. For instance, you don't really have to worry about how many people show up at a gig. You could be backing up someone who has a disastrous turnout at a venue and thus no chance to ever play there again, but this won't keep you from playing the same venue next week with a different performer.

Be professional. This should be obvious, but it always bears repeating. Show up on time, or better yet, early (it doesn't matter how good your excuse is, you're losing points if you're late). Make sure you carry extras of everything you need.

Don't do anything that makes more work for your boss, and if possible help out. Performers have lots to worry about at gigs and you shouldn't be adding to their worries in any way. You should be responsible for everything that involves you. If you ask for a set list and there isn't an extra for you, copy it yourself. If there is no set list at all, don't press the issue. Let the sound engineer know what you'll need. Be cool. Make the phrases "no problem" and "that's fine" a major part of your vocabulary. Many sidemen end up also serving as guitar techs for performers. If this is something you feel comfortable with, you'll rack up a lot of points by doing things like tuning up the performer's guitar and even taking care of their sound check yourself.

Unless the performer has a set place for you to stand on stage, make sure you set up in a place that will let you see the performer's hands (if they're a guitarist) and hear whoever else you feel you need to hear—bass player, another guitarist, etc.

AT THE GIG

So now you're on stage and you're wondering what to play. This is always the most difficult thing about being a side musician. How much do you unobtrusively support the performer, and how much do you inject your own personality into the proceedings? Many great musicians are terrible at communicating what they want from the people they play with. The best way around this is simple: ask. If you're wondering whether you should be supporting their rhythm playing or playing fills incessantly, just ask them which they prefer. Even if you've had no rehearsal and little time to communicate, ask them between sets if they like what you're doing. They may not even know (many people don't know what they like until they've heard it), but at least they'll know that you're trying.

Pay attention at all times. Even if you've memorized arrangements perfectly, things always change on stage. The performer may forget the words to a verse and go into a chorus early. If you're paying attention you'll hear it; if not, it'll sound like *you* screwed up. Be ready to solo at any moment. Some performers will turn your way and nod when it's time for you to let your fingers fly, but others think that staring at their fingerboards and closing their mouths is an appropriate mode of communication. Endings are easy to anticipate. You just have to be listening. Most last notes are the downbeat of a measure and you just have to be ready to not play the second beat when you reach the end of the song.

So you're soloing now. Should you pull out those 32nd-note seven-octave runs you've been practicing all week or simply play an unadorned version of the melody that drips with sustain? Most performers will tell you that they love tasteful guitarists, but the fact is that you don't want to become a faceless entity. If you have a musical personality, don't hide it. Don't start showboating, but let your natural musicality come out. For one thing, you'll get bored very quickly if you're just being anonymous. And if the audience likes your playing, you'll become an asset to the show. Finally, don't wait until you feel like you've got the gig to show them how you play. If you start out playing in one fashion, they'll expect to hear that every time and be surprised when you finally reveal your true nature. Besides, if they don't like your playing, you don't want the gig anyway.

To some it may sound like being a full-time accompanist is like being a glorified roadie in constant danger of playing a wrong note. But the rewards of being a side musician are great. It keeps you "in the moment" and never lets you revert to autopilot. It's likely you won't have to figure out how to make a song sound fresh the 500th time around. There's also an odd satisfaction that comes from adding something to and improving a song that you'd prefer never to hear again. Oh, and one more tip. No matter what musical disasters may befall you, always look as if you're having the time of your life and absolutely mean to play every note that stumbles out of your guitar. I once was asked to play an intro to a song I'd never played before. I got a little flustered and started the tune a half step below the key of the song. When the band came in I just slid up a fret and continued to play as if nothing was wrong. After the set, someone came up to me and said, "Wow, that lick you played at the beginning of that last song was amazing!"

Getting Paid

David Hamburger

Most people feel that money is a somewhat private affair, and everyone has strong feelings about the relationship between money and art, so it's no surprise that the issue of getting paid can be a complicated one for musicians. Even if you play music strictly for fun, or you're in a band where everyone shares the expenses and plows the income back into the group, you may find yourself negotiating on your own behalf at some point. If you audition for an already existing band, get called to play on a demo or CD project, or get asked to go out of town for some gigs with someone you've been backing up around town, you're going to need to have a discussion about getting paid.

Getting paid is a matter of arriving at an agreement that satisfies both your expectations and the other party's resources in a realistic way. After a weekend out of town with a band I used to work in, the bass player would hand me a roll of bills and say, "Here you go. It's less than you deserve and more than I can afford." One relatively polite way to find out in advance what the fee is going to be is to ask, "What's the budget like?" This works better for recording projects than for gigs, because everybody knows it's going to cost something to step into the studio and plans accordingly. This question also acknowledges that you know they don't have an infinite amount of money but that you assume some of that cash has been earmarked for what you do.

For a live gig, there may be a guarantee or set fee offered to the band by the venue—the club, festival, or wherever it is you'll be playing. Keep in mind, however, that you're being hired out of the band's general resources, and if the venue is paying X amount of money for a five-piece band, you may not necessarily be getting one-fifth of that amount. The band has overhead, like any other business—travel expenses, mailings, maybe its own PA, and so on. In fact, as a side musician, you *are* one of the band's expenses. Remember also that a band that guarantees a flat rate to its side players usually loses money on some gigs, because it has to hire people for gigs that pay little or no money but benefit the band in the long run.

You yourself have to weigh how much a gig or session is worth doing based on the amount of exposure it will give you. At the beginning, it may make sense to do things for less money in order to build up your track record and your reputation. At a certain point, it's good to establish some kind of rate just to clarify that what you do has value. And the more experienced you get, the more you're worth—the better you know how to prepare for a gig, the quicker you can get acclimatized in the studio. Many people don't realize the intangibles you bring to the table that make you worth what you're asking—maybe you're already familiar with most of the country standards the band plays or you're able to make your own accurate charts before the session. You can explain that these things affect your rate.

Dobro man David Hamburger.

And there are certain intangibles that *you* get from doing gigs, things you might consider if the money seems meager. It's certainly more persuasive to approach a venue on behalf of your own band if you've played successful gigs there with another group (but do it with sense and tact; don't point out how your band would make the perfect replacement for the folks you've been doing regular Thursday nights with for the last month and a half). And any time you get yourself on tape, it's another example of your work that you can give out when someone wants to hear what you're able to do. If the music is actually coming out on a CD and might get some airplay or a review, so much the better.

Setting rates for yourself has a lot to do with context. What are other people charging for similar kinds of work? There isn't much standardization in the music world, but you can determine certain things by asking around. Again, people can be weird about money, but if you're getting into situations involving pay, there are probably at least a few people around who you know well enough to talk to. And you'll get a feel for the going rates once you start having these kinds of negotiations. There will always be gigs you do just for the hell of it, and there should be. The best part of knowing what you're worth and commanding a certain degree of respect is choosing, once in a while, to play the gig or make the session just because it sounds like a good time.

Sound Decisions

Harvey Reid

Harvey Reid works out on his Dobro guitar.

It might be feedback squealing all through your quiet song. Or you might not be able to hear yourself. Your voice and instrument may not be balanced properly, or you may be in a group and unable to hear the other members. Anytime you walk out on stage, ready to play music, sound problems can completely defuse your performance.

The easiest response, and one that many seasoned professionals employ, is to blame everything on the equipment or the soundman. This does not help the audience hear any better and creates bad politics at the gig. If you and your instruments are properly prepared for each performing situation, you can do a lot to make sure that you spend your time on stage playing music and not fighting with sound.

Deciding what specifically to do and what equipment to buy depends on a number of factors: the kind of music you play, the instruments you use, the volume level you want, and the performance setting itself. There are so many variables and tastes that no simple answer or piece of equipment will make you sound good in all situations. Yes, folks, this means that you will have to learn something and make agonizing and expensive decisions—you won't be able just to learn or buy the answers. What follows is an overview of some of the choices you'll have to make.

Unless you are lucky enough to perform only for quiet groups in acoustically excellent rooms, you will have to use a PA system for performances. Even concert halls that have been built specifically for music listening tend to be designed for operas or symphonies and are really too large (in spite of what anyone says) for a truly effective performance with just an unamplified acoustic guitar.

Those of us who play and enjoy music must learn to cherish those times when we have a great acoustic setting—at home, at a party, at the beach, or at a bluegrass festival out in a field with the bass thumping through our feet and the sound of all the instruments and voices projecting through the air like magic. And we must learn to accept all the shortcomings and trade-offs that come with the use of a sound system. Only a few people can crowd around the bluegrass band in the field before the sound that reaches outer listeners becomes muffled and changed. With the use of amplification and recording, many more people can share in the experience of the performance. Although an amplified performance or a recording can never capture the true spirit and content of the music, it captures something of value. Every person who performs or enjoys music must decide how picky they wish to be on matters of "purity" and reproductions. Some people are happy just listening to a small kitchen radio, while others have compact disc players in their cars and are still unsatisfied. If you've never been in a small room with a skilled musician playing a quality instrument, you've missed something. But it also is undeniable fun to listen to your favorite song on your Walkman as you walk through the woods or to be at the concert, even if you are in the back row.

Looking for "natural" sound is not really the point; what you are looking for is good sound. And the decision as to what is good is maddeningly subjective. In a quiet coffeehouse, all you need to do is mic your guitar and make sure you are behind the speakers to minimize feedback. But if you try to mic a Martin D-35 with a Shure vocal mic, such as they use at most coffeehouses, you will not get the best results; in order to get the maximum stage volume you'll want the guitar as close to the mic as possible, but directional mics (almost every mic you'll ever encounter; the opposite of omnidirectional mics) have a property known as the proximity effect that means when you get the sound source closer to the mic, the bass response increases. Singers love this, but it makes a guitar, especially one with lots of bass like a D-35, roar and rumble excessively in the PA. So you need to EQ the mic to remove some of the bass or choose a mic that is better suited to the instrument's sound. Mics designed for vocals have an EQ curve built into them that makes singers sound better but that can make guitars feed back.

Now this same setup might make you completely happy at the coffeehouse, and it might give enough volume for a lounge gig at the Holiday Inn, but there you run into some other problems. Because the last 20 people who played that gig all had pickups in their guitars, and because the kind of music you would be expected to play at a Holiday Inn lounge relies considerably on signal processing, you would simply sound wrong to the audience if you tried to do the gig with your Martin and your Shure mic. And it would be a fashion thing more than anything: you would sound like a coffeehouse performer. And a mic signal run through a chorus box or compressor sounds horrible.

So you might decide you need a pickup to get more volume and that modern sound. There are several types of guitar pickups: magnetic pickups that fit into the soundhole, piezo-electric pickups that attach to the body of the instrument, and piezo-electric pickups that fit under the saddle. For sound and convenience you might think about installing a preamp and control knobs on the guitar. Then again you might not want to drill holes in your 1956 Martin, and you might just want to use an endpin jack and use external controls. More decisions. The best answer depends on what you need or can afford rather than on some world standard.

You might like the natural sound of a mic and want to use a mic and a pickup together on stage. This is often an excellent choice, but if there are five people in your group and all want two instrument channels and a vocal mic, you need a 16-channel mixer and a 30-minute sound check for even a short showcase gig. Or if you use wireless gear, you'll need two wireless units at double the expense and bulk, and double the risk of something going wrong. You might want to install a mini-mic inside your guitar. This adds volume and convenience but causes some new wiring problems and can be expensive if you use several instruments on stage. If you play in a band with a drummer, a lot of your choices are made for you. You pretty much have to give up the idea of miking the guitar because of the stage and monitor volume, unless your band's PA can allow you to send only the pickup signal to the monitors and the mic and pickup both to the house. At extreme volumes you might even have to stuff your guitar with towels to lessen its resonance and feedback.

The point is, if you want to be heard you might as well do your homework and keep informed of the best way to amplify yourself. New equipment comes out every year. Ignoring the problem doesn't make it go away. Musicians who spend years learning to play their instruments often don't realize it is of almost equal importance to learn to use the sound system when performance time comes.

Choosing not to deal with the issue is still making a passive choice, and failing to use your PA properly still makes a statement to the audience, just as you make a fashion statement when you dress sloppily. You might be playing great music or speaking deep truths, but if the mics are feeding back and the tweeters are blown in your speakers the effect of the truth and music may not be felt. Another performer with a great sound system and less truth is likely to connect better with the same audience.

The more that you the musician understand what is coming out of the speakers, the more effectively the whole music will come across to the audience. Artistic decisions underlie all the technical talk, and artists should make them.

Amplifying Your Guitar

Chris Proctor

Perhaps you can recall the climactic scene from the movie *The Shining,* in which the crazed homicidal Jack Nicholson character pursues his poor, unfortunate child into an overgrown maze, complete with all of the usual dead ends and blind corners, and the audience watches in horror as Nicholson draws closer with each mistake of his prey.

The guitar owner in search of the perfect way to amplify his or her guitar might well feel some of the same desperation as that boy. In the amplification maze, you'll find dozens of product options, each claiming to be an acoustic-electric breakthrough, and an accompanying thicket of information and misinformation. And the ogre who represents bad sound, bad feedback, bad advice, and bad choices is ever at your heels.

On the other hand, there have been technical advances in recent years that bring closer the elusive goal of good amplified sound, and there are players in all acoustic genres who are pointing the way toward the Holy Grail of guitar amplification—a way of making your guitar louder without feedback, and a way of doing so that brings across the qualities you value in your guitar sound to whatever audience you seek.

There are tools available to help you make sense of this search, and questions to ask yourself that can help to point you in the right direction. The tools are straightforward:

First, your chosen guitar, set up as you prefer, with newish strings of the type and gauge that you normally use.

Second, a good musical-instrument dealer with a wide knowledge and range of products, who has an in-store sound system for you to test your options. The most helpful dealers are willing to answer questions and open packages, and they are candid in telling you what they don't know or don't have in stock, so that you are exposed to the widest possible range of choices.

Solo guitarist and composer Chris Proctor.

Third, a PA system, amp, headphones, or home stereo where you can do more evaluation and fine-tuning outside of the store.

Fourth, an inquiring mind.

Now the questions, also four in number.

How much trouble are you willing to go to?

If you are already experiencing that sinking feeling that you get when a project looms and threatens to overwhelm you, you should stop here, buy whatever your dealer initially recommends, your buddy uses, or you can find on sale, and settle down to practice Neil Young's solo from "Down by the River." You can always come back to this chapter if you get dissatisfied later.

The rest of you are now forewarned that work and learning lie ahead, and that the fix might not be clean and simple. I'm suggesting early on that you might not be able to simply go to your dealer, purchase a reputable, easy-to-use product, mount it and use it as advertised, and be completely satisfied with the sonic result. The guitar is a difficult beast to amplify well, as we shall see, and this quest may get complicated.

How much are you willing to spend?

This question is related to the first one. Guitarists have options ranging from $30 to $1,000 or more, and you will need to know your budget before you start. Allow room in your budget for other gear that you will need to purchase after you decide on a pickup or microphone, including but not limited to preamps, cords, equalizers, power modules, direct boxes, and effects. If you don't know the meanings of any of these terms, please check the definitions below.

How loud will you need to be?

Are you going to play in your living room, perform at occasional open-mic nights at local coffeehouses, make a living in a variety of performing situations, play at outdoor festivals with loud monitors and mains, play in a band with other amplified electric and/or acoustic instruments . . .? The louder you need to be, and the bigger your audiences, the more critical your choices are, because flaws in your system tend to be exposed by higher volumes, by higher audience expectations, by comparison with the sound quality of other performers, by additional feedback potential, and, of course, by Murphy's Law.

STARTER QUESTIONS

How Much Trouble Are You Willing to Go to?

Hardly any trouble	*Some trouble*	*Lots of trouble*
External mic Simple soundhole pickup Simple stick-on or saddle pickup	Internal mic or pickup Factory-installed mic/pickup combination Simple preamp or EQ	Complex dual-source system Effects, mixer, outboard preamp

How Much Are You Willing to Spend?

$30–100	*$100–300*	*$500 and up*
Inexpensive pickup or microphone	Higher quality mic Internally mounted pickup Basic on-board preamp	High-quality condenser mic Dual-source system Sophisticated outboard gear

How Loud Do You Need to Be?

Home alone	*Open-mic night*	*Local hero*	*Professional*	*Road warrior*
Microphone	Simple pickup	Internally mounted mic or pickup	Combination of sources	Complex dual-source system Parametric EQ, outboard gear, graphic EQ, mixer, effects

What Type of Live Sound Do You Seek?

Natural acoustic sound	Acoustic-based with electronic influences	Alternate amplified reality

What kind of live sound do you seek?

Do you tend toward the traditional natural-as-possible side of the spectrum, or do you find yourself attracted to larger-than-life or alternative-reality guitar sounds? Are you committed to maintaining the acoustic sound you achieve in your living room, or are you eager to use newfound electronic colors to paint a picture that bears little resemblance to that acoustic sound? Of course, there's a large middle ground, inhabited by players who base their amplified sounds on their acoustic ones, but who choose to alter them with some electronic spices. Keep in mind, too, that an amplified sound will never be the same as a pure acoustic sound, and it may or may not be true that a so-called "natural" amplified sound will work best for your purposes.

INSIDE YOUR GUITAR

Now let's talk about your guitar. The guitar presents problems in amplification for several big reasons. It produces sound in three different ways—from the strings themselves, the vibrations of the top, and the air moving from the soundhole—and it's important to pick up the sounds from all three of these sources when you make the instrument louder. The guitar's large and sensitive top is also quite good at picking up vibrations from the air (from a speaker, for example) and creating a feedback cycle. The feedback problem is ever present in discussions of amplification; it is the major reason that pickups exist in the first place: as attempted solutions to the inherent limitations of sticking microphones in front of instruments and cranking the volume up.

So far, technology has provided us with five amplifying methods.

EXTERNAL MICROPHONES

Ah, the good old days, when this was our only choice! On the good side, they are far and away the most faithful-sounding single option, they require no internal mounting in your guitar, and you can change the quality and volume of the sound by moving your instrument into different positions. The bad side, however, is often very bad—feedback when you turn up loud enough to be heard; howling, booming bass when you get too close; and the distractions in your mind that these possibilities cause. Also worth considering are the difficulties of remaining rooted in front of the mic when you feel like hopping on top of your Marshall stack during the finale, and the possible distaste you might feel for having a barrier of highly chromed, visible mic stands between you and your audience.

John Renbourn plays into a pickup and an external mic. Below, the B-Band system's internal mic.

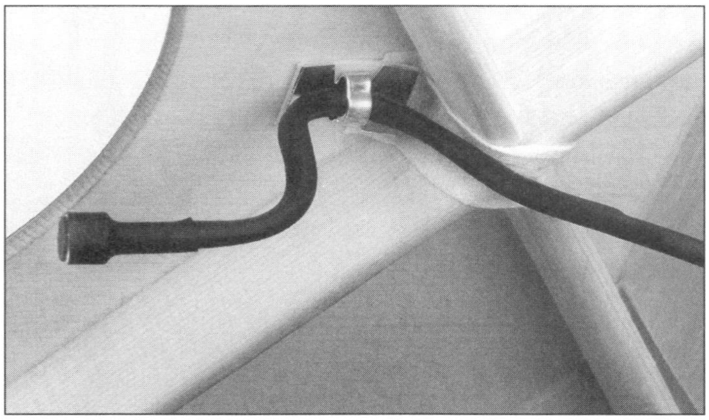

If you decide to go this route, choose a quality microphone with a tight (usually called cardioid, hypercardioid, or unidirectional) pattern, which tends to reproduce sounds from the front and reject those from the rear. Look for a condenser microphone made specifically for performance use. To decrease feedback, you can eliminate or turn down your monitors, remove the offending (usually bass) frequencies from the main or monitor speakers with equalization, and experiment with your location in relation to the mic and speakers so that feedback decreases. Use your sound check time wisely: go early, when no one is there to be disturbed, and experiment with every idea that occurs to you. A good microphone and some good equalization equipment, along with knowledge of the gear and a strategy for using it, will make it possible to get most of the qualities of your guitar out to your audience most of the time in small, relatively quiet settings.

INTERNAL MICROPHONES

There are a lot of these available now, and they improve on the feedback problem of external mics, improve on the stationary problem, and still give you a sound that is quite close to that of external mics. Drawbacks . . . Well, some would say that quite close is not close enough and that acoustic purity demands an external mic. Internal mics also must be installed inside the guitar by a qualified person, and they often require phantom power, meaning that your mixer or a box you plug your mic into must provide power. (Most mixers and preamps *do* provide phantom power.)

Internal mics require trial and error for maximum sound and minimum feedback, and there is still a good chance that you'll encounter situations where you can't get enough gain before feedback rears its ugly head. For most users, the perimeter of the soundhole, with the head of the microphone facing in toward the center, is a good starting location.

PIEZO-ELECTRIC STICK-ON PICKUPS

These pickups attach to the top wood, usually inside the guitar in permanent installations, and amplify the vibrations at the point of attachment. Obviously, the choice of that

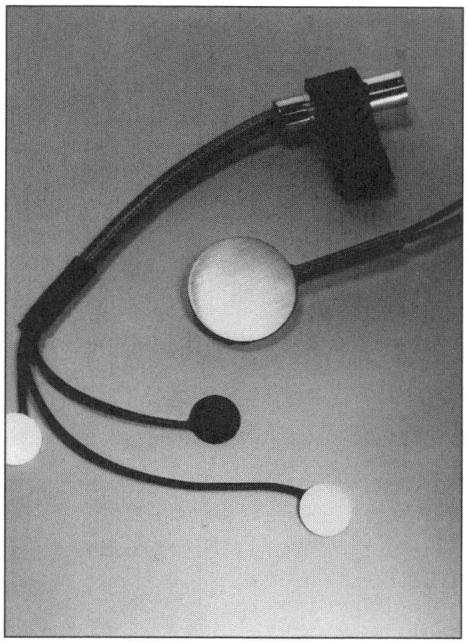

Seymour Duncan stick-on pickups.

location is a biggie. On the positive side, you can fine-tune the sound by moving the pickup until you find a sweet spot on the top that yields a sound that accurately represents your instrument. On the negative side, you have to take all of the strings off the guitar to move the pickup. You will also find that your choice of mounting material (double-stick tape, superglue, epoxy . . .) affects the tone, and that feedback is still possible, since that sweet spot you found in your experimentation may be a sweet spot for snagging stray sound waves from the air as well.

A suggested starting point for attaching these pickups is on the bridge plate (the reinforcing piece of wood that lies opposite the bridge and saddle inside your guitar) in line with the B or G strings. Put the pickup as far away from the bridge pins (toward the lower bout of the guitar) as you can go. Most of the models currently available are very user friendly, with instructions and tips, adhesives and Velcro for isolating cords inside, and dedicated endpin jacks already wired up.

Use whatever mounting substance the manufacturer provides, and don't glue the pickup in unless you're sure that you will like the result! Some pickups come with internally or externally mounted battery-powered preamps as well. Stick-on pickups are generally extremely high impedance, which is another way of saying that your preamp needs to be close to the pickup to protect the quality of your signal. Trust me and buy a short, high-quality cord (five to ten feet) to run between your guitar and preamp. Internal preamps for these pickups are currently being designed and should reach the market before too long, and they will make it possible to use a longer cord without signal loss.

TO INSTALL OR NOT TO INSTALL A PICKUP

Q *I want to put a pickup in my guitar, but I fear that its acoustic tone will change. Should I worry about this?*

A I generally tell my customers not to put pickups into their most precious acoustic guitars if they are at all concerned about changing the instruments. I also advise them to go ahead and do it if they really want to use the instruments on stage in situations where a mic just won't do.

It is very reasonable to have two or more instruments, using one for stage performance and preserving the best for purely acoustic playing. Yes, perhaps drilling holes will lower the rate at which your instrument will appreciate over time; we now look very favorably upon archtop guitars from the '30s and '40s that have never been sullied by pickups. As for tone and volume, I've been involved in putting bridge pickups in hundreds of guitars in recent years with only one complaint of tonal change. A well-done installation will not affect the structural integrity of the instrument.

—*Rick Turner*

UNDER-SADDLE PICKUPS

Under-saddle pickups are the market leader, and with good reason. They are out-of-sight, require only minor alterations to your guitar, can be very loud without feeding back, and aren't too expensive. What are their drawbacks? Well, they can sound bright and midrange-heavy, lacking both the extreme high-end sheen and the rich low end of the acoustic instrument. Also, they make it difficult for you to adjust the saddle height, since the pickup either is the saddle or lies directly beneath the saddle, making a shim sort of problematic. Some folks feel a little uneasy about placing anything at all between saddle and bridge, feeling that this might compromise the acoustic tone.

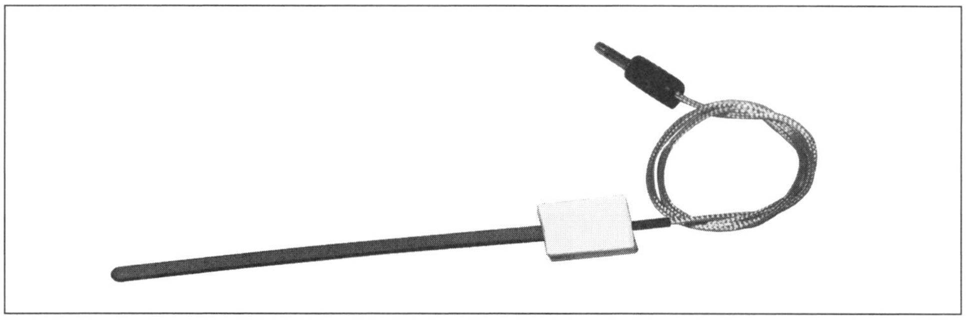

An L.R. Baggs saddle pickup.

Unlike with a magnetic pickup (see below), you'll need to buy a saddle pickup without truly knowing how your guitar will sound until the installation is complete. Make yourself as comfortable with that fact as you can by listening to other installations of similar pickups in guitars similar to your own. Most models include an internal, battery-powered preamp as part of the installation.

Under-saddle pickups cost $100 and up, not including installation, and packages with external preamp/EQ boxes are available for those who want more sound-shaping power. Make sure that your installer has plenty of experience with the pickup you choose. I think that most players with saddle pickups will want some external EQ, and a budget of $200–$350 is not out of line for the whole package.

MAGNETIC PICKUPS

These products are usually suspended in the soundhole, using a magnet to amplify the strings moving above. Because these pickups are isolated from the moving air and body wood, they are very feedback free, and they also work best of all of the choices for techniques like right-hand tapping or slide, which sometimes generate undesirable body or handling noises when miked or amplified with saddle pickups. You can also slide the pickup in and out as the need arises without altering your instrument.

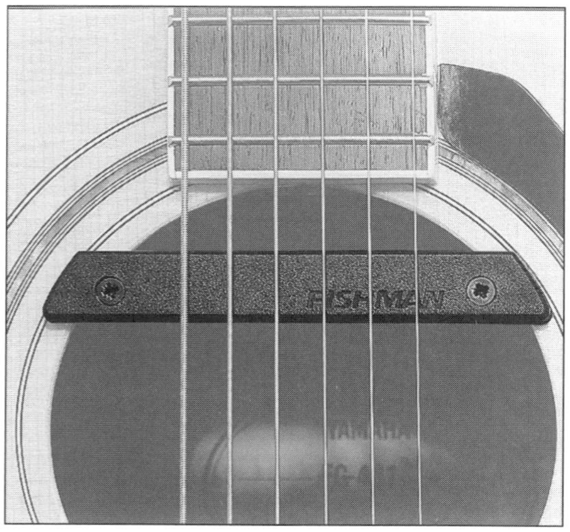

Fishman's Rare Earth magnetic pickup.

On the downside, magnetic pickup output won't sound a whole lot like your guitar unless you're willing to equalize it, and bronze strings can sound unbalanced when used with a magnetic sensor that is only capable of responding to steel. The latter problem gets especially dicey with a 12-string guitar with plain-steel octave strings paired with bronze-wrapped strings. The plain strings will sound louder, and sometimes quite strident, when you are playing fingerstyle.

You can cope with these imbalances by experimenting with equalization, moving the polepieces up or down on the adjustable types, and using strings like GHS White Bronze, which are engineered for a more even response in such situations. My observation has been that relatively fresh strings are more important for a good mag-pickup sound than they are in any other setup. There are many models commonly available, and they range in price from $50 to $200 and up, so experimenting before you buy is thoroughly advisable.

IS THAT ALL THERE IS?

Heck, no! You may have chosen your pickup or mic with the help of all of these wonderful insights you've been given, and you may be bursting with desire to plug in and have at it. But did you notice how none of the products were described as perfect, without drawbacks? Those of you who carry this search to the professional level will grow dissatisfied with any one single product, no matter how well made it is. This is the guts of the matter: Amplification can't be done easily if you need or want it to be done well.

Many players, especially professionals, have needs that can't be satisfied by one amplification device, and they assemble personalized combinations of amplification devices and outboard gear. Why do so many players choose to thus complicate their musical lives? Feedback and bad sound—sound that doesn't communicate what they want and need to communicate to an audience.

MULTIPLE-SOURCE SYSTEMS

Solo guitarists in particular have come to embrace systems that involve more than one pickup or mic as the most high-fidelity means to reproducing guitar sound on stage. Any two sources with different approaches—such as a microphone and a saddle pickup—will

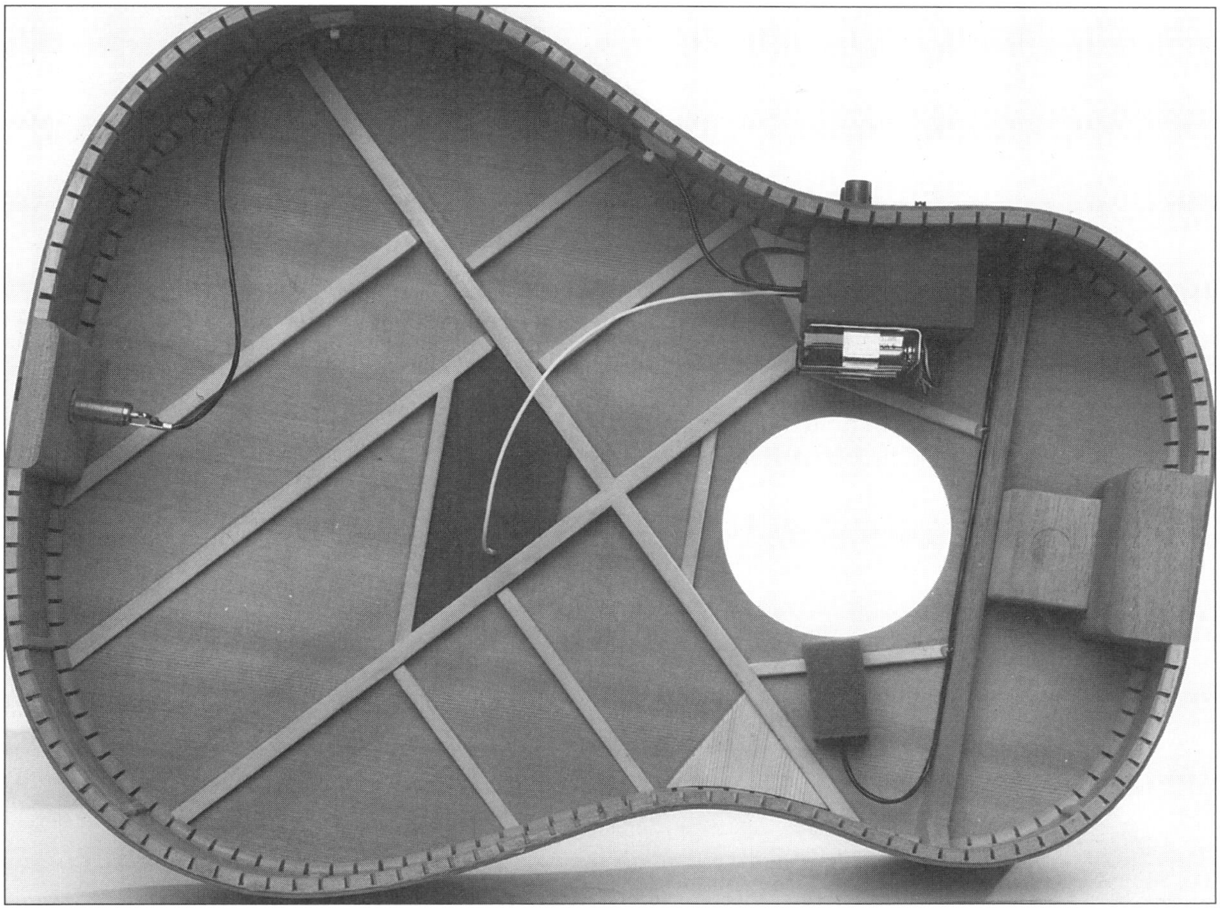

The Baggs Duet mic/pickup system, with preamp and controls on the upper bout.

work well together. Each takes a different picture of the guitar's sound and fills in the sonic holes that the other creates. A good combination is a magnetic pickup and a stick-on or saddle-mounted pickup. Microphones can also be blended with magnetic pickups in do-it-yourself applications, and a few companies market them together in easy-to-install packages. Pickup and guitar manufacturers have been working together to reduce the size of multiple-source systems and to have them factory-installed.

A common package is the mic and saddle pickup with tone, blend, and notch controls installed into the upper bout of the guitar where the performer can easily make adjustments. These systems generally position the microphone inside the guitar's body aimed at the soundhole. Manufacturers generally choose this spot because it's a happy medium—the placement that satisfies the most guitar players. Because they need to make things compact and easy to install, they have fewer options than does the experimental guitarist sitting at home with PA, pickups, and soldering iron in hand. So, the question is whether you want to go for the factory- or store-installed package and hope that it does the trick, or set out on the long, somewhat expensive, and certainly time-consuming quest for great sound, a quest that will need to be repeated from time to time as amplification products evolve. Many on-board installations commit you to today's technology and to one particular application of it.

Manufacturers are making better products every year. What happens two years from now when there's a mic, pickup, or preamp you like a lot better than the one that's inside your guitar? How do you feel about cutting a hole in the nice rosewood sides of your guitar, a requirement of some integrated systems? These questions make the case for external gear and for removable pickups. Another big issue is equalization. What happens when you realize that you would like to equalize the microphone differently from the pickup, or the magnetic pickup differently from the piezo? Most of the factory-installed

USING EFFECTS

Q *Do most people performing with plugged-in acoustic guitars use some sort of effects? What do they use?*

A The most common effect used with acoustic guitars is reverb. It puts the dry, direct sound of a guitar's pickup into an artificial acoustic "room" or "hall" to help it sound more natural. It can also be set to add sustain to finger-picked styles.

Natural acoustics will vary as you go from one room to another. A lush reverb that sounded great on headphones or in your living room may make the instrument sound far away and indistinct in a bigger room. And too much of any effect can be worse than none at all. I recommend using subtle effects that can barely be heard. This way they will support the performance rather than overshadow it.

Chorus can be a pleasant effect as well. Chorus mixes the direct signal with one that's been delayed for a few milliseconds. The length and depth of the delay are adjustable. Chorus usually makes an acoustic guitar sound like a 12-string. The chorus effect is roughly analogous to swinging your head back and forth while playing acoustically in front of a hard wall. The common tool is the chorus pedal, which is small enough to fit in the neck of your guitar case or the pocket of your gig bag and requires only one extra cable and a spare battery.

Serious gearheads like to use rack-mount multi-effects units that can produce a wide range of different effects—echo, reverb, chorus, distortion, compression, and equalization—and can store different combinations as presets so they can be called up at the touch of a button. This feature allows you to cross over from an acoustic to an electric sound without changing guitars. Each song's effect can be tweaked and then stored as a preset, allowing you to step through them using a foot pedal, thus eliminating the need to fiddle with any controls. The advantage to having all these effects at your disposal is that you can control how and when they will be used. You can simply tell your sound system operator that you will take care of all your own guitar effects from the stage.

Shop around for effects and be wary of used ones—there's a good chance that they're difficult to use or sound bad. And remember, the more time you spend playing with effects, the less time you're actually practicing or writing songs. However, if you have an extra Franklin or two (as in Ben), then perhaps a little technology will inspire you to do more with your music.

—Mark Frink

systems have a combined output, with no ability to equalize the two sources separately. If you have a magnetic pickup and a microphone, for instance, you will want to use tone controls to shape the magnetic pickup's sound to take advantage of its strengths and cut away or minimize its weaknesses, and you might also want to apply a notch filter or other tone-shaping device to the microphone. You won't be able to do that unless you can somehow divide the two sources and send them through separate signal processing chains. Most on-board installations don't allow you to do this.

Two pieces of information tend to reassure those who choose on-board dual systems: First, some manufacturers have committed to sizing all future design improvements within the current standard preamp footprint and shape, so that you can purchase a new model of dual system and have it installed in the same location in your guitar without any additional cutting or modification. Second, new dual systems are under development that will allow you to select the standard on-board mono blend or a new external stereo blend that would use a stereo-to-dual-mono Y cord in the endpin jack. This choice would make it possible to use the simpler approach with a blended output, or to bring the two sources out separately and equalize and mix them externally for more professional requirements.

EXTERNAL BLENDING

External multiple-source systems are on the cutting edge of guitar amplification. The evolution of the gear is relatively fast paced, the costs are somewhat higher than those of on-board systems, more experimentation is required, and there are fewer informed sources to use as guides, but there's no doubt that the results can justify the labor involved. The general do-it-yourself plan is this: Install your two sources and wire them to a stereo endpin jack so that they share the ground but have separate hot leads on the tip and the ring portions of the jack. Then plug a stereo male quarter-inch cable into your guitar. This cable will run into a dedicated preamp like the Fishman Blender, Rane AP-13, Pendulum SPS-1, Raven Labs Master Blender, or Boss AD-5, which will divide the signal into its two separate sources and give you individual control over the tone, volume, and effects for each pickup. Another way to achieve the same goal is to physically split the cable or use a splitter box to do so and send one pickup into one channel of a mixer and the other into another.

If you're considering modifying your existing amplification system, you can add a second source, but chances are that your existing endpin jack won't have any open terminals. Most of today's saddle pickups use the third terminal on a stereo jack to turn the internal nine-volt battery on and off when you insert a cable, so you'll have to do some fancy rewiring to add the new pickup or microphone in a way that doesn't leave your battery on all the time. Of course you can drill a second hole for endpin jack number two or dangle a wire out of the soundhole, but who likes those solutions?

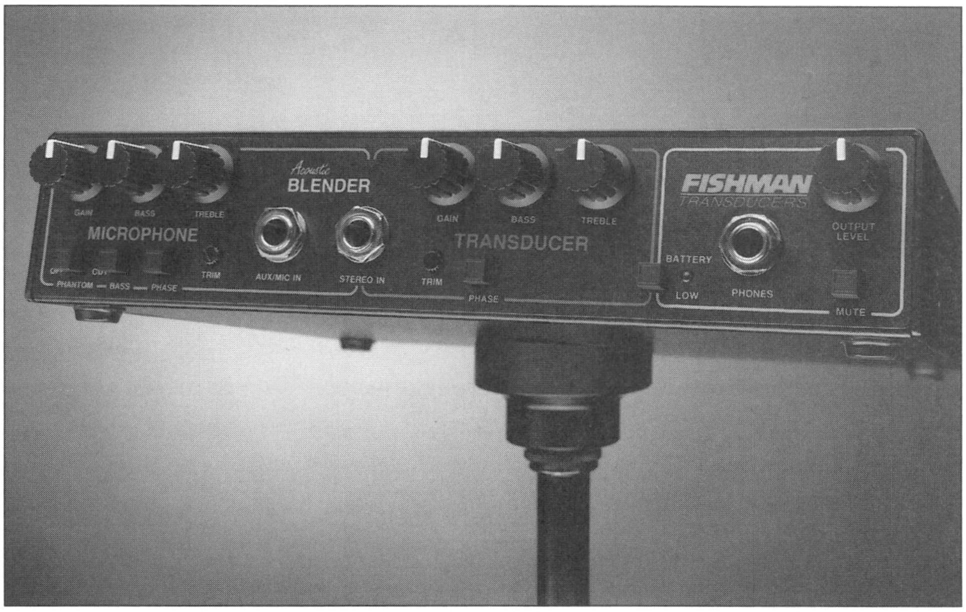

The Fishman Blender mixes and matches mic and pickup signals.

Manufacturers are addressing this issue. A four-conductor endpin jack, such as EMG's UltraJak and Fishman's Switchjack, allows you to install a saddle pickup with an internal preamp and still have at least one free terminal on the endpin jack to add a second source that is separable outside of the guitar. You could add this fact to the list of arguments for using external and replaceable gear: when improved products hit the market, you can use them.

If you do choose to combine pickups and/or mics on your own, you will end up needing outboard gear to equalize, mix, and effect the signals to achieve your goals. You will need to investigate what gear will phantom-power your mini-mic (since it carries no battery power of its own), boost your weak pickup signal, buffer it to lower its impedance, equalize it to eliminate feedback or choose the part of its sound that you wish to use, add effects to it, make it stereo or mono, and send the final product off to be amplified. If you can have your gear close to you on stage, you'll make different choices than if you must stay a long way from it, but the products fall into several broad categories in either case.

PREAMPS

Preamplification devices boost the relatively weak and high-impedance guitar signal so that it is more able to survive long cables. Some of them also offer tonal control. Internal preamps, often no larger than three or four inches across and usually powered by single nine-volt batteries, are usually dedicated to the pickup they're designed with; so you must take care if you keep your preamp but switch pickups, because the new source may have properties for which the preamp has not been engineered and equalized. External preamps allow you to experiment easily with different options, and there are several products like the ones mentioned above made specifically for the multiple-source crowd. The units can get complex. They are

SIGNAL LOSS

Q *Does it degrade the pickup signal at all to run it through extra stages, like an electronic tuner or a volume pedal?*

A This is a tough call. In general, the fewer the stages, the better the sound. Tuners generally have buffered inputs that are parallel to the signal and should not load the signal down. Some effects have hardwired bypass switches so that the signal only goes through the electronics when the effect is on, but some run the signal through a stage of electronics even when they are off. Volume pedals can have a sound-altering loading effect on signals depending on the source. The effect isn't too bad on preamped pickup signals; it's a bit more noticeable on unpreamped magnetic pickup signals and even more so on unbuffered piezo pickup signals, which really need preamping before they go through anything more than a few feet of cable. Even "passive" components, such as cable and volume controls, have an audible effect on signals.

I recommend that you use your ears as test instruments. Try using the fewest stages of electronics possible, then add one thing at a time and see if you can hear insertion losses or signal degradation. Audiophiles with high-end stereo systems are so concerned with loading the signal that they sometimes forego tone controls. The best tack is choosing the right pieces of gear to begin with so they do not require a lot of tweaking or audio Band-Aids to sound right.

—Rick Turner

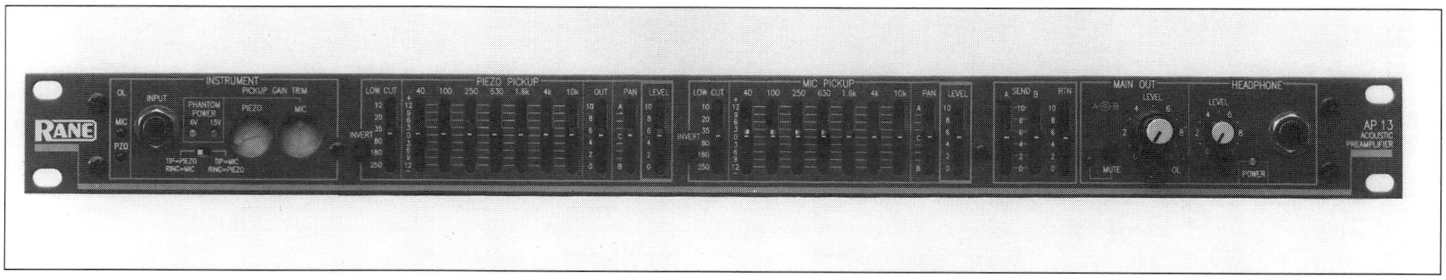

Rane's AP-13 is a rack-mountable stereo preamp with many blending and equalization features, plus phantom power.

often AC-powered, and some are rack-mountable; they may offer built-in parametric and/or graphic EQ, effects loops, stereo capability, and the capability to handle two sources, sometimes from one stereo cord. They usually provide an output called line level, which is a signal of greater strength, similar to that of the outputs of professional sound reinforcement products like mixers and effects devices. A line-level signal is directly usable as an input to a power amplifier. (Note: Internal preamps do not produce a line-level signal.)

DIRECT OR BUFFER BOXES

These devices are intended to transform the guitar's signal into a lower impedance signal that can survive the trip from the guitar to whatever lies ahead in high-fidelity form. These boxes are good choices for people who stand a good distance from their electronics when they play (more than six to eight feet) and people who want to run their signals directly into the house sound system. Some of these devices have gotten more complex, with extra capabilities similar to preamps. A well-made box of either type will do a good job, and they come with or without batteries.

Direct boxes intended for professional use can be expensive, and sometimes relatively heavy, AC-powered affairs with high-quality tube circuitry, and many pickup users swear by the sonic improvements they hear with this tube gear. A common use of the tube direct box is with a high-quality magnetic pickup, but in fact tubes tend to warm up the amplified sound in any pickup application. They are definitely a little more expense and trouble, and they are a little more vulnerable to rough handling than solid-state boxes or preamps.

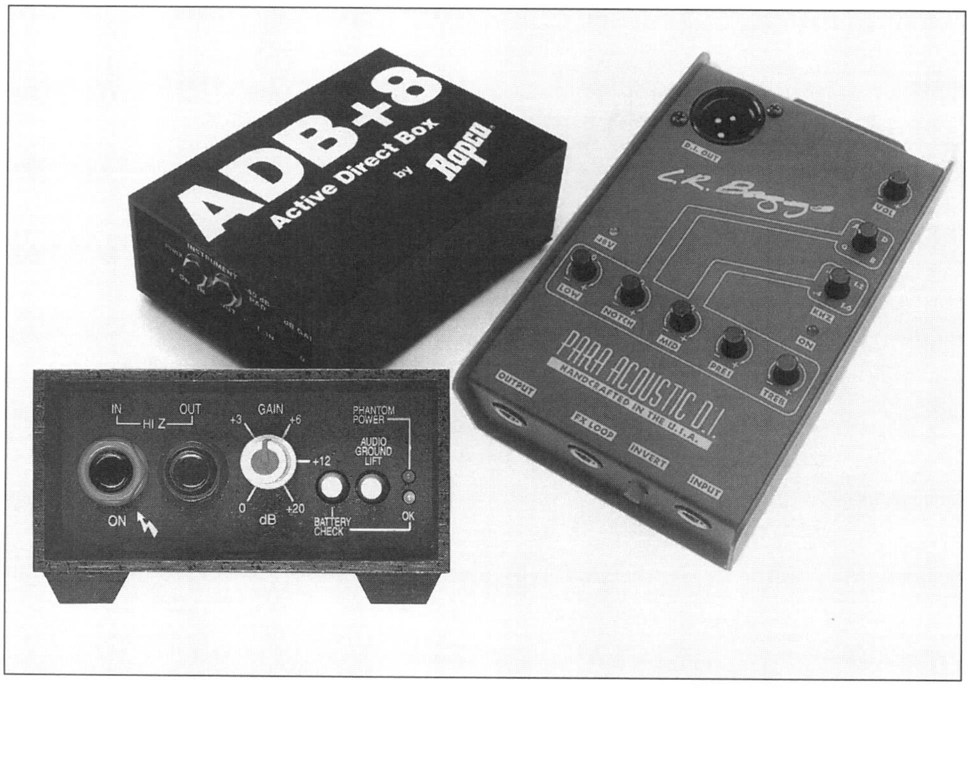

Direct boxes from ARX, Rapco, and L.R. Baggs.

EQUALIZERS

Equalizers give you the power to dramatically alter the quality of your signal by cutting or boosting specific frequencies. There are two types of equalizers: graphic and parametric. Graphic equalizers provide the user with easy-to-read sliders to cut or boost in specific ranges, usually from one-third of an octave to two octaves per slider. These equalizers give the user a great way to shape overall sound. Parametric equalizers offer knobs with which you can select target frequencies, choose how wide or narrow an area around a target frequency you wish to control, and cut or boost in that specific area. They are wonderful tools for eliminating specific problem areas, such as feedback on one segment of your bass response or the midrange bite so often created by saddle pickups. All guitar tops have specific resonant frequencies that are very prone to feedback, which occurs somewhere around 200 hertz. Parametric or notch filters are the tools of choice to eliminate that oversensitivity, without throwing away much baby with the bathwater in the process. Graphic equalizers are usually better for general problems and deficiencies in the overall sound, and they are easier to use in performance.

This Boss pedal offers simple graphic EQ. The Fishman unit below features parametric EQ.

NOTCH FILTERS

A notch filter, which is often included in higher end preamps or amps, is a precise antifeedback tool and a valuable addition to your amplification arsenal. Rather than shaping the overall sound, it performs selective surgery on problem areas in the mix.

The human ear can hear about ten octaves of sound on a good day, ranging from thuds and low organ notes at around 20 cycles per second (or 20 Hz in sound engineer parlance) to barely perceived and whispery sibilance and cymbal overtones at 20,000 cycles per second (20 kHz). When you reproduce or amplify sound and want to alter the natural quantities of the various tones you're dealing with, you are equalizing the sound. If you're listening to rock 'n' roll on the car stereo and the music is too boomy, you turn down the bass, which is a very crude way of equalizing the sound. It's crude because you only have two knobs with which to influence those ten octaves of sound—bass and treble—and when you're turning the bass knob down you're turning up several octaves at once, not just the three- or four-note span that's probably causing the problem.

Let's say you have a microphone inside of your acoustic guitar and you've amplified that mic and guitar through your guitar amp until it's very loud. Your guitar is a sensitive beast, and the top begins to pick up the vibrations emanating from your amplifier. The microphone picks up the vibrations and sends them back to the amp, and presto, you have major feedback. What do you do? The equivalent of turning the bass knob down, which will eliminate the feedback but will also make your guitar sound like a trebly and brittle shadow of its former self? Reduce the volume, so that no one in the club can hear your playing? No, you pull out your notch filter.

Unlike the bass knob on your car stereo, or even the ten bands of equalization available on many mixers and amplifiers (one for each octave), the notch filter is preset to cover a very narrow spectrum of frequencies (about one-sixth of an octave, or about two notes' or two frets' worth of signal) and to cut those two notes rather severely, without cutting any other tones. Chances are that your guitar has one very sensitive pitch that makes it feed back relatively easily. Just crank the volume knob until the feedback occurs and then sweep the notch frequency. Cut that frequency, and your guitar will keep its rich sound without feeding back. You can also use a notch filter to tone down any annoying midrange bite (usually around 1–4 kHz) created by your under-saddle pickup. Crank up the volume and fish around a little bit with the notch filter until you've found and removed the problem area.

SMALL MIXERS

These instruments try to be all things to all people by combining some of the traits of all of the gear discussed above. They have four to 12 separate channels, each with some capability to change impedance, equalize, boost the signal, create stereo or mono options, insert effects and additional equalizers into the signal path or at the final outputs, and provide strong, line-level output for amplifying. Many players use small mixers to provide phantom power for their internal microphones as well, and some products are specifically engineered for two-pickup configurations or combination pickup/mic setups. As with any piece of equipment that combines functions, mixers can't always perform each function with the detail of a dedicated piece of gear. But the advances in technology that are making mini-mics and preamps better and smaller are doing the same thing in the field of mixers.

Mackie's small but powerful 1202 VLZ mixer. Below, Roland's Boss AD-3 processor, designed for acoustic instruments.

EFFECTS

The final elements you might want to put into your signal path are effects. Some professional guitarists believe that reverberation is the irreducible minimum that an amplified acoustic guitarist needs, and some feel that chorusing is a very good way to broaden the often sharp attacks that pickups produce, and that a chorus or enhancer effect at an almost subliminal setting are just as important as reverb. Where do you fit on the "natural versus alternative reality" scale? If you prefer microphones and want a minimum of electronics in your signal, you might omit effect entirely, whereas the sky is the limit for you experimental types. You'll have to choose from pedal-type effects (which are usually noisier, battery-powered, lower fidelity affairs, and less expensive as a result) and rack-type effects (which are higher in fidelity, price, features, and flexibility).

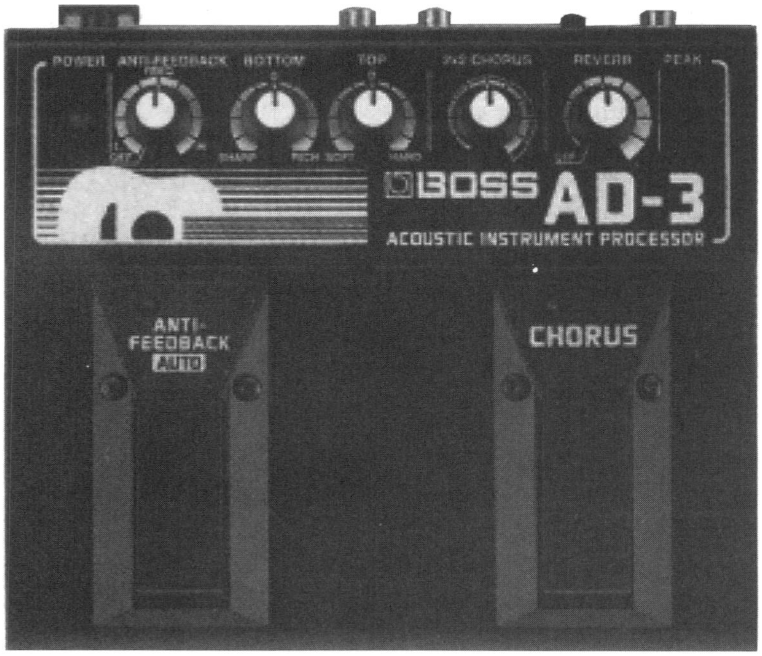

Please be aware that plugging your precious guitar signal directly into a pedal effect is a very quick way to degrade the signal and reduce the eventual quality of your sound. Effects loops, wherein your guitar signal is first preamplified, then sent in a separate, controllable path into one or more effects units, is a far cleaner and more professional way to achieve the same objective. Most high-quality, performance-oriented audio products will offer you one or more effects or auxiliary loops that enable you to do just that.

ACOUSTIC AMPS

There are many kinds of acoustic amps now available, and they're popular for a reason. An acoustic amp is a PA in a box, often packaged with additional features acoustic players find handy, such as notch filters, phantom power for internal mics, and digital reverb. While the traditional PA comes with a separately powered mixer (or mixer and power amp), two speakers, and cords to connect the various parts, the acoustic amp combines all of these parts in one portable box. Some are absolutely spartan affairs, with one quarter-inch input, minimal EQ, no effects, and one speaker. High-end amps usually include some of the effects we've discussed, woofer/tweeter/crossover systems for better fidelity, as well as bal-anced/XLR and unbalanced quarter-inch inputs, and they give the user the ability to mix and equalize these sources independently. They generally range in price from $300 to $2,000. Some players use acoustic amps to process their dual-source guitar signals and to act as stage monitors. They run a balanced, premixed line to the house system but keep the amp on stage to ensure a consistent sound.

Drawbacks to acoustic amps? Remember that there are reasons why traditional PA systems exist. For every casual gig where a guitar amp provides more than enough volume and much greater ease of setup and use, there is another situation in which you'd

Fender's Acoustasonic SFX combo amp.

SOUNDHOLE COVERS

Q *When I see bands live, I often notice that the acoustic guitars have black covers over the soundholes. What are these for, and who makes them?*

A Many acoustic guitarists who are competing with electric instruments at high volume levels use soundhole covers on their pickup-equipped instruments in an attempt to combat feedback. The idea of covering up the openings of a guitar goes back to jazz players seeking ways to play louder with their feedback-prone archtops. Some of them resorted to inflating balloons inside their guitars or filling their guitars with scraps of leather, although strips of tape over the f-holes is the more common solution.

Given that a flattop's sound comes from the entire top, rather than just out of the soundhole, covering the soundhole has less of an effect than you might think. But every little bit helps, and in some cases the few extra decibels gained by covering the soundhole make the necessary difference. Kaman Music Corp. offers two different soundhole covers designed to fit most standard-size guitars. The Silencer is made from durable plastic and features an adjustable opening for creating the desired tone. The other unit is the Feedback Buster, a simple, round rubber plug.

If you've got an odd-shaped or -sized soundhole that won't accommodate an over-the-counter solution, you might try this advice from guitar maker Rick Turner on making your own custom cover. "Use some black plastic such as Stewart-MacDonald's #1030 (.06-inch thick), available in a 12-inch by 20-inch piece from Stewart-MacDonald [(800) 848-2273; www.stewmac.com]. That will give you and your friends feedback suppressors galore. You can cut this plastic with a heavy-duty pair of scissors and smooth the edge with a file or emery board. Cut a piece in the shape of the soundhole about 3/16 of an inch too big. Get some 3/8-inch or half-inch adhesive-backed, closed-cell foam (used for weather-stripping and gasketing). Cut four 3/4-inch strips of the foam and slightly undercut a ledge approximately 1/8 inch by 1/8 inch from the adhesive side. Adhere the foam blocks to the back of your soundhole cover in such a way that the foam will fit snugly into your soundhole and the wooden edge of the soundhole will lodge into the ledge or slot."

Guitarists who rely on internal mics for their sound might find that covering the soundhole changes their amplified sound quite drastically. As with all things related to acoustic amplification, experimentation is the key.

—Teja Gerken

POP-FREE CABLES

If your guitar has a jack to plug it in, one obvious accessory you'll need is a cable. By using a unique shorting pin, Switchcraft's Silent-Plug quarter-inch phone plug (catalog number 181), which attaches to the guitar end of the cable, you can eliminate that annoying thump when you unplug. This is especially helpful if you change guitars often throughout your set. It also calms the audience's nerves during long, multi-act festivals, and the sound people will think it's magic. No more hand-waving at the end of the set when you want to unplug. Guitar players can quietly unplug at will, without giving any notice. Switchcraft's quarter-inch plug number 182 also has a built-in rubber washer that clamps down on the cable to relieve strain. The people who work at your local music store may have to special-order these items, but you'll be doing them a favor by turning them on to these parts, and if you can't solder, they can probably put one on a cable for you.

—Mark Frink

love to have speakers distributed in strategic locations in the room. Acoustic amps are often placed on the stage next to the performer, ensuring that the player will be focusing that fine acoustic amplified sound into the kneecaps of the audience rather than into their ears. As you approach high volumes, feedback becomes more likely if you're relatively close to your speakers than if they're on stands 20 feet away. If your speaker is also your mixer, and you need to adjust volume and tone occasionally, that speaker can never be placed far beyond your reach, and that fact can become a liability in larger rooms. If your performing sights are set higher, you will eventually want the greater bass and volume capabilities of separate speaker enclosures and larger power amps, as well as the capacity for stereo separation, which makes effects much more realistic. For these reasons many performers opt for separate components. One popular setup that combines elements we've discussed is a guitar with two sources installed inside, a two-rack shoulder bag containing one of the dual-input preamps and an effects device, and a small PA system with a vocal mic, two speakers, the necessary stands, a six-channel powered mixer, the appropriate connecting cords, and, of course, a home-equity loan application.

MAKING YOUR CHOICE

So how do you make sense of all these options? For one thing, revisit the questions that we posed in the beginning of this chapter. When you're investigating amplification gear, talk to other players about their experiences and be as well educated as possible. There is no substitute for a good music store and some critical listening.

Bringing Your Own Microphones

Mark Frink

As a solo troubadour, you must be self-reliant, equipment-wise. Once at the gig, the gear you've brought is all you'll have to solve any of the sound system du jour's shortcomings. I like the two-hands rule when it comes to deciding what to bring. Obviously, the guitar goes in one hand. Your other hand carries the product-and-wardrobe case. Everything must fit within the confines of this baggage, or you'll need an extra hand.

Along with the gear specific to your instrument (strings, capo, picks, tuner), there are several small audio accessories that can be helpful to have at most shows. My suggestions include one or two microphones and maybe a direct box. Other important bits include Sharpies, batteries, foam windscreens, blank cassettes, and cables. I advise marking all your stuff with colored electrical tape, using the same color for everything you own. This way you'll have no trouble identifying who owns what, especially when sorting out mics, cables, and DIs at the end of the gig. Small, foil return address labels are an inexpensive way to help items left behind find their way home, and etching your social security number on all your road pieces to thwart thieves is also a good idea.

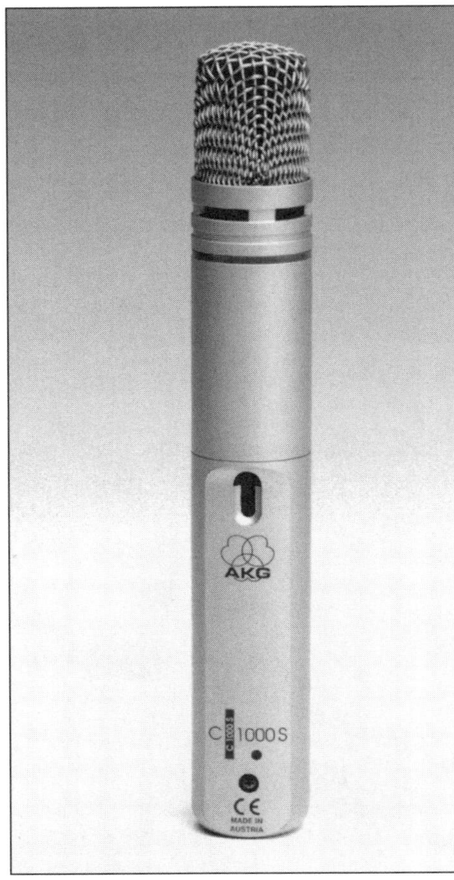

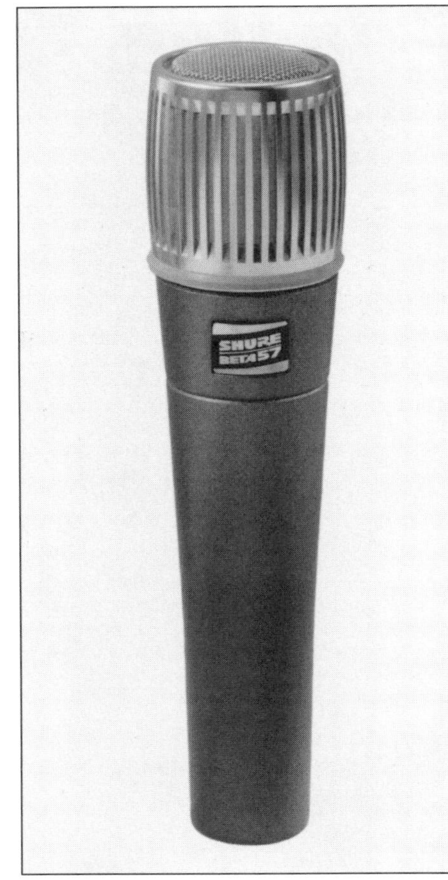

AKG's C 1000 S condenser mic and Shure's Beta 57 dynamic.

Why go to the trouble and expense of bringing your own microphone when most venues supply them? There are several good reasons. When you bring your own vocal mic, only *your* lips need to be on it. Also, your mic probably sounds better than the club's, even if it's the same model. Thirdly, it gives you an excuse for dedicating your own channels on the mixing board, helping to preserve the settings from sound check until show time.

CHOOSING A MIC

There are basically two kinds of microphones: condensers and dynamics. Condenser mics, which are generally more expensive, are commonly found in recording studios and require phantom power to run their built-in amplifiers. This voltage—specified as 48 volts but in practice often lower—is supplied from the console directly through the mic cable. Condenser mics are not always your best bet. Some smaller mixers cannot provide phantom power. Other reasons to avoid condensers are that unplugging a mic that uses phantom power causes a loud pop when the channel isn't muted, and that certain problems with mic cables allow dynamic mics to work but prevent phantom power from operating. Lastly, extreme moisture (a likely condition at those rain-or-shine outdoor festivals) can cause condenser mics to fail. All in all, while condenser mics often sound better than dynamics, success in the marginal situations that abound at coffeehouses and smaller clubs can be achieved by bringing a good dynamic mic or two. Dynamic vocal mics usually require different EQ settings than condensers, and since most small venues provide dynamics, substituting your own dynamic is relatively simple for the sound engineer to deal with.

The most common dynamic mics for live sound are the Shure SM58 for vocals and the SM57 instrument mic. These are nearly identical except for the 58's ball grille. Most sound techs are familiar with them and know how they work with their sound systems. Though

ALL AROUND THE MIC

The unique sound and dynamics of early bluegrass bands were influenced by the way the musicians positioned themselves around one microphone, and in recent years, some traditionalists have been experimenting with a return to this minimalist approach to amplification. Mainstream audiences received their first exposure to the one-mic technique at the 1998 Farm Aid concert when Steve Earle and the Del McCoury Band performed to 25,000 people while clustered around a single Audio-Technica 4033 condenser mic.

Using one microphone for an entire group of singers and acoustic instrumentalists may sound like a soundman's nightmare, but Earle says, "We had a little feedback when we started, but Ray Kennedy, who coproduces all my stuff, wrestled it to the ground pretty quickly." Playing in such a tight configuration removes the need for on-stage monitors, the source of most acoustic feedback problems, and also creates a striking natural choreography. "When I was a kid, the thing that most impressed me about watching bluegrass bands was the choreography involved in working one mic," says Earle. "I always thought that was the coolest thing in the world to watch." It's a definite improvement over watching a line of stone figures staring at their fingerboards.

Mike Bub, bass player with the McCoury Band, says, "Nowadays everybody gets in front of their microphones and there they stay. It's hard for an audience that's trying to follow everything on stage. Like, for the mandolin break, you have to look over there and watch the mandolin player. And sound people have to do the same thing. They don't know what's coming next so they're always chasing your solo. With one mic, you watch the center point and the music comes to that."

Steve Earle and the Del McCoury Band circle around a single mic.

Nonbluegrass artists such as acoustic country duos Gillian Welch and David Rawlings and Jones and Leva have also tried the one-mic approach. "We find that we sing much stronger and more naturally because we can hear each other," says James Leva. "We also match vocal tones better."

"Everything blends together more naturally up there," says Bub. "You don't have all of this processing that's changing all the instruments into some new thing that comes out of a speaker in front of you. And it's great for singing."

So how does the one-mic approach sound to the audience? No amplification approach is foolproof, but when the one-mic setup is used well by the musicians and the engineer, each instrument and voice is clear and distinct, the natural dynamics are vivid and exciting, and the blend has the air and shimmer inherent to acoustic instruments.

Of course, it isn't a case of just plug it in and go. I've heard some disastrous initial attempts. Like anything else, doing it right takes practice. Choreography is the most obvious thing that musicians who decide to investigate the one-mic approach will have to learn. "The first time we did it, I was real proud that I got through the whole gig without putting Del's eye out," says Earle. "It's actually pretty simple. The banjo and the mandolin and the fiddle work in a circle, and everybody else just stays out of their way. Ron [McCoury] and Del were telling me, 'Just remember, go to the left.' And it works. Playing this music, I'm now more comfortable with the one-mic thing than I am being individually miked. It's really fun to do. It's the most fun I've ever had playing music, period."

—Scott Nygaard

many clubs provide Shures, their condition can leave much to be desired. Using dissimilar mics on a sound system can lead to differences of tone quality and even feedback problems. When bringing your own SM58, you ensure that EQ adjustments made for the club's 58s will be compatible with yours, making changeovers easy and trouble free. Using the same kind of mic for both your vocal and your instrument means that EQ settings in the monitors that work for one will help keep the other from feeding back.

Even better are some of the newer microphones that offer refinements on the 58, including Shure's Beta 58 and Beta 57, which can both be used for vocals. There is also Audix's line of vocal mics. The Audix introductory-level OM-3 can be found at many music stores, as can the OM-5, which has a fuller and brighter sound, and the smoother-sounding OM-6. All of these mics behave similarly to the Shure 58, but with extended highs and better gain before feedback because of their increased directionality. The best test, of course, is your own ears. Compare one dynamic mic to another by simply speaking into one and then quickly unplugging and trying another mic on that same cable. You can compare mics in the store, and some some shops will even let you take them home overnight to audition.

As I mentioned, bringing your own mic gives you an extra reason to ask for your own dedicated channels in the PA. The same mic stand and cables can still be used by others by simply jumping the XLR connectors over a couple of channels. Just make sure they're changed back for your set. Setting aside your own channels helps guarantee that your sound-check settings will be preserved until your performance. This is even more important when it comes to having your own instrument mic or DI, since guitars can vary more widely in tone and volume than voices. The only other settings you'll need to ask to have preserved for you are the master EQ for the monitors and mains and perhaps the reverb setting.

JODY STECHER ON MIC TECHNIQUES

The biggest problem I've noticed in sound reinforcement for acoustic guitar is the absence of a mental picture of what it should sound like. Often the sound engineer has a vague and mistaken idea based on the so-called "unplugged" piezoelectronic snarl. An engineer cannot get it right without having listened to the performer's guitar the way it is played by the performer, which is what ought to be done as a starting place.

In my own case, tone and sound are very important, so I usually want something approaching accuracy, allowing for the inevitable acoustic differences of each performing space. But often I get an alternate version of sonic reality that is reasonably pleasing, so I go with that rather than wasting time. If I find that I have a situation where the engineer cannot or will not give me a clear and deboomed sound, I will back off from the mic most of the time and then use the proximity effect from time to time to give my bass notes an exaggerated heaviness that is big fun in certain situations.

Make sure, if you are using mics only, that the "smiley face" EQ pattern that is appropriate for DIs and for a rock band is corrected. The beauty of a guitar is mostly in the midrange. Don't let the sound setup remove the mids or you will find no beauty.

I've had the best sound from condenser mics, especially when the engineer knows how to use them. Generally the bass has to be rolled off, for instance. A Neumann KM 84 can be lovely with some bass removed. I've had good luck with a variety of AKG mics. Two that come to mind are the 460, which does a good job at the sweet spot (usually below the part of fingerboard that lies over the body) and the C 747, a hypercardioid mic that picks up the entire face of the guitar. Dynamic mics can be fine. They are also easier to use. There is nothing wrong with a Shure [SM]57, but the [SM]58 is a crummy guitar mic.

WINDSCREENS

Foam windscreens for vocal mics lessen the percussive breathing effects of close-miked vocals and reduce "P-popping." They only cost $5, look nicer than the nylon-stocking filters used in studios, and provide the extra benefit of preventing lip contact with strange foreign matter found in the mic grilles at some clubs. By resting your lips on the foam, you maintain a close distance to the mic without having to actually kiss it. Small differences in mic distance make a large difference in volume. When you halve the distance between the mic and its sound source, the level increases fourfold. Twice as close to the mic turns it up by 6 dB—the equivalent of going from a 100-watt to a 400-watt system. Also, the closer you are to the mic, the more lows come through, making your voice sound bigger and warmer. And when used at outdoor shows, windscreens offer the intended benefit of cutting back wind noise.

PLACING A GUITAR MIC

If you're using an external mic on your instrument without a pickup, you must carefully position both to get the best sound. First, make sure the back of the microphone points toward the floor monitor, because this offers more gain before feedback. This is your best hope of hearing your guitar over the clinking coffee cups or beer mugs. Now, which part of the guitar gets the front of the mic?

Try an experiment with the help of a cooperative sound engineer. Wearing a pair of headphones plugged into the mixing board allows you to isolate the sound and hear what the different placements of a microphone offer. Putting the mic down by the bridge can be dull-sounding, but moving it too far toward the neck can produce a thin tone. Many people think that the sound comes out of the soundhole, but that's not the (w)hole story. With many guitars there's a spot about halfway between the shoulder and the soundhole, near where the neck meets the body, that is full and balanced. As you experiment, you'll discover that changes in position of only a few inches can have a dramatic effect.

Finding a good spot and maintaining it can be quite frustrating as it divides your attention from the performance you're giving. If you're sitting, it's pretty easy to get that mic to stay in one place, but if you stand up, you'll want to be able to move with the music. Try standing in front of a mic with your guitar strapped on in its usual spot. Think of a song that makes you want to move. Loosen your knees and shake your hips. Without moving your feet, swing your guitar back and forth and move the neck up and down as you might during a raucous tune. You'll notice that the same spot between the upper bout and the soundhole hardly moves at all (Elvis knew this). If you put a mic right there, you can waggle like crazy and still get a consistent sound. You also want to keep the mic as close to the guitar as possible without bumping. And a second windscreen will be forgiving if you bump the mic with your guitar.

PA System Basics

Mark Frink

Performing musicians who work without the aid of a regular sound engineer develop a sound-check routine, a standard sequence of procedures that is their foundation for achieving optimal and consistent operation of a sound system whose controls are in the hands of a different person for each gig. Before we get into the components of that routine, it is helpful to be familiar with the names and functions of the controls of a typical sound system, most of which live on the control surface of the mixing board. In this chapter we'll start with the sound equipment, and in the next we'll talk more specifically about the steps to take during sound check.

MONITORS

The biggest decisions are made around the use of floor monitors, or *wedges,* as the sound techs often call them. Some solo acoustic players even perform without a monitor, and this simplifies things. If there are no speakers pointing directly at the microphones from a few feet away, the sound system is less likely to feed back. Performing without monitors allows you to listen to what's happening in the room from the stage and get a better idea of what the audience is hearing. Placing yourself close to the audience puts your ears in closer proximity to the audience's sound field and helps those in the front row hear you better. The main speakers to either side can even be moved back a bit or turned in slightly to improve your ability to hear. You may be surprised at how this technique puts you "into the mix" if you are in the right kind of room with a polite audience. If you haven't tried it before, though, keep in mind that this approach is not for those with shy voices or timid technique. It works best in "live" rooms with reflective surfaces like wood, plaster, glass, and brick. It also works better in situations where people have come primarily to listen to music, rather than drink and chat with others. If you are outdoors, in a room with lots of carpet and drapery, or competing with food and alcohol service, you may be better off with a monitor.

In situations where you need monitors, the critical decisions involve balancing the sources that are dialed into them, and blending that with what can be heard from the main speakers and the room. Some prefer to listen to just the monitors first, while others will start with the mains. The limiting factor is the microphones, so these should get adjusted first, before the pickup.

MIXERS

Sound systems with single mixing boards have many controls in common that suggest a logical sequence to achieving satisfying results quickly. Monitors in smaller sound systems are run from the same mixer as the main speakers. The monitors are mixed from an *auxiliary bus*—one knob for each channel in a row above the faders—that combines different amounts of signal from each input and is separate from the main mix. Back in the '70s, when all sound systems were run from a single mixing board, the monitor mix was called the *foldback* because it consisted of signals sent from the console back up to the stage. Nowadays large concert systems used on tours and at bigger outdoor festivals have a separate mixing board at the side of the stage dedicated to controlling the monitors.

If you're not familiar with them, the knobs on a mixing board can seem intimidating. Relax, it's much simpler than it looks at first glance. Keep in mind that even on the largest mixing boards, once you learn the first column of knobs for a single input, each additional input is identical, so all you really need to learn is one input's controls and the rest are just more of the same. Let's quickly review the four types of knobs on an input channel.

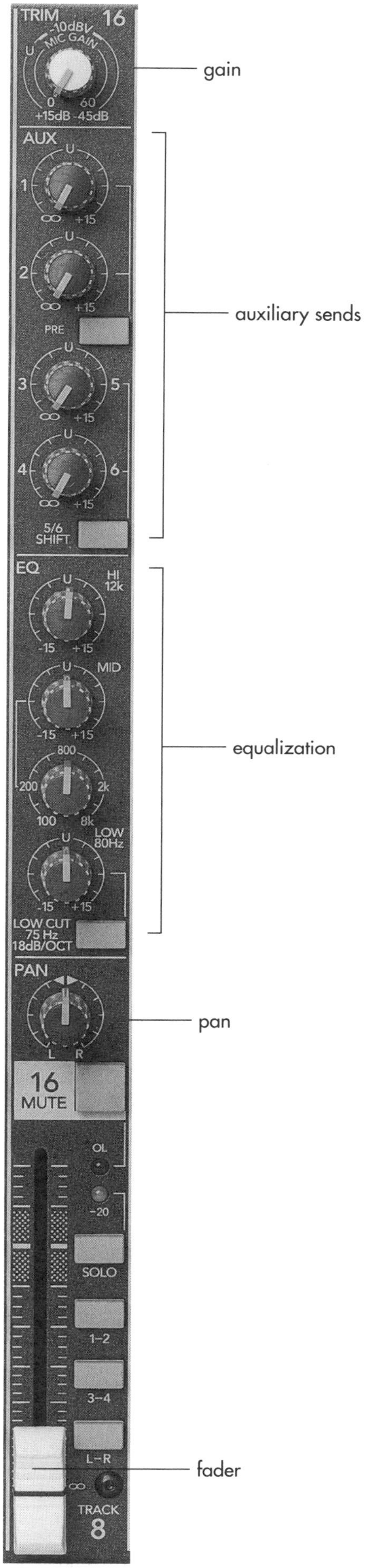

LEVEL AND PAN CONTROLS

At the top of each channel is the *gain,* the knob that controls the input's preamp, which is the first thing the mic or DI from the stage hits when it arrives at the board. This is adjusted so that the console has roughly equal signals to work with. Louder or "hotter" sources, like drums or guitars with built-in preamps, need less gain. Quieter sources need more gain. At the bottom is the final level control, usually a fader, which determines how much of the signal gets to the main mix. Just above the fader is the *pan* knob, for adjusting the signal's balance between left and right on the main output of the mixer.

EQUALIZATION

Above the pan knob are the knobs for tone control, called *EQ* for equalization. Usually there are three or four. Just like the bass and treble controls on your stereo, there is an adjustment for lows and highs. Between them are knobs that control the midrange frequencies, or mids. The exact frequencies that these knobs control are not as important as your familiarity with what they do in a general sense. The lows are usually around 100 cycles per second, or 100 hertz, affecting the lowest notes on your guitar and the warmth or boominess of your voice. The mids are where the harmonics of the guitar start, usually around 1,000 hertz, abbreviated 1 K by sound techs. These midrange frequencies are what you hear over a telephone, the middle of the frequency spectrum. Using fewer mids can help the signal sound more hi-fi, and more will give it the ability to be understood better, since these are the tones the human ear is most sensitive to. The highs are way up around 10K, helping the voice's sibilance and the squeak of guitar strings. The highs are sometimes referred to as *presence,* and using more can make something sound closer, but too much can sound unnatural.

More sophisticated mixing boards have what are called *sweepable mids,* allowing the midrange frequencies affected to be tuned to higher or lower frequencies. This is good for acoustic music, because many acoustic instruments need adjustment in the low mids—closer to low frequencies, but not quite there. Many guitars benefit from having low mids turned down to reduce a "boxy" or hollow sound without losing the fundamental tones from the lowest strings. Voices can benefit from adjustments to the upper midrange, or high mids. Some singers have a hot spot in their upper register that needs to be cut a little, and some vocal mics need a small boost or cut in the high mids to smooth them out.

The important thing to know is that all these EQ changes made on the main speaker mix do not affect the monitors on many single-mixer systems. With this design, your operator is less likely to cause feedback, except by turning the signal in the monitors up too loud. This has a couple of implications that we'll get to when we consider a good approach for our sound-check routine.

AUXILIARY SENDS

This brings us back to auxiliary-send knobs, or *aux sends* for short, which are used to send the signal (along with other inputs whose knobs in that row are turned) someplace other than directly to the main mix. There are basically two uses for aux sends: to send the signal to a monitor amplifier, or to an effect, such as reverb. Effect sends are usually *post*—their signals are derived after both the EQ and main mix level, so that changes to the main mix fader and EQ also affect the signal being sent to the reverb. This is because the reverb is returned to the main mix, and the signal sent to the reverb usually needs the same level and EQ changes the main mix gets. Monitor sends are what is called *pre*—their levels are not affected by changes to the main mix or by EQ changes on the channel. Some mixers have pre-fader aux sends that *are* affected by EQ changes to the main mix. This makes it important to make EQ adjustments to the mains before setting the monitors.

GRAPHIC EQ

The overall tone of the monitors is usually controlled by a single equalizer, the *monitor graphic*—a menu of tone controls on sliders, spread over the entire frequency spectrum. If your vocal mic needs to have some frequencies reduced on the monitor graphic to sound good, this will also reduce those same frequencies in your guitar in the monitors. If your vocal mic has frequencies that need to be cut so it won't feed back, those frequencies will get cut from your guitar, too. If the graphic is used to make an acoustic instrument sound better, those changes will affect the vocals in the monitors as well. It is wise, therefore, to use the graphic primarily for the vocal mic, since there is no other way to control its tone, and to compensate for the changes made to the sound of your guitar with a separate tone control, as discussed below. A good approach is to start with a musically pleasing setting on the graphic at a low volume and then bring the level up a little more and deal with specific frequency areas that are feeding back. It is important to correctly identify the offending frequency to cut, rather than pulling many out at once.

ON-STAGE CONTROLS

Having a separate tone control for your acoustic instrument is becoming more common. Controls similar to the mixing board's lows, mids, and highs can often be found on either the instrument itself or on a separate preamp box. This allows you to optimize the vocal mic in the monitors with the monitor graphic and then use the guitar's tone controls to get it to sound reasonable in the monitors. Newer versions of preamp boxes combine the balanced outputs found in DI boxes with a sweepable or *parametric* midrange that allows the tone to be better tailored to a specific acoustic instrument.

PUTTING THE PIECES TOGETHER

While this may sound complicated at first, with practice it becomes as simple as tuning a six-string. Making the right initial moves and using a good strategy will get you the results you want, as long as you have decent sound gear and a cooperative operator. For the solo performer, there are rarely more than three inputs: the vocal mic, the instrument mic, and the DI. There are only three places to send these three inputs: the mains, the monitors, and the reverb. There are often just three tone controls on each channel. There will be plenty of voice and instrument in the mains, but the real challenge is getting workable levels and balance in the monitors.

Taking time to get familiar with the controls on small mixers will help you to ask for what you want when someone else's hands are controlling the knobs. Most sound engineers are happy to spend a few minutes showing you what they know and how the different controls affect the sound system. They know that the better you understand what they're doing, the easier it is for them to make you happy with the sound. Getting to the gig a little early will give you a little more time to learn about sound. Start by just playing a CD through the system and checking out what the different knobs do. Watching and listening to someone else's sound check can also be informative, so if there is someone else playing on the bill with you, ask the sound engineer if you can look over his or her shoulder.

ROOM ACOUSTICS AND FEEDBACK

The shape, furnishings, and size of the venue have a significant effect on feedback. Hard surfaces and low ceilings increase the likelihood of feedback. Parallel walls and ceilings that are parallel to the floor can lead to the production of a standing wave, a particular note that bounces back and forth between the parallel surfaces producing a peak that can lead to feedback. Loudspeaker placement relative to your position in the room and the volume at which you play become even more significant if the room is working against you.

There are a few things that can help. For example, try to avoid pointing your speakers at hard reflective surfaces (or the bartender). Avoid placing your speakers (or yourself) in the corner of a room. If you find yourself in a small club and you have to turn down (because of feedback) to the point where the people in the back cannot hear you, try running a spare amp or speaker right out into the room. Reasonably priced, powered extension speakers are available. This method covers a larger area with less volume and can increase audio fidelity, but in bigger venues it can lead to audio-delay problems. If the stage floor is boomy when you tap it with your foot, it's all the more important to try to keep your amp and/or speakers up off the stage. Try placing your amp on a chair with something soft like a cushion under it, or if your amp is heavy, some thick, soft, rubber feet may be a good investment.

—*Bob Wolstein*

Creating a Sound-Check Routine

Mark Frink

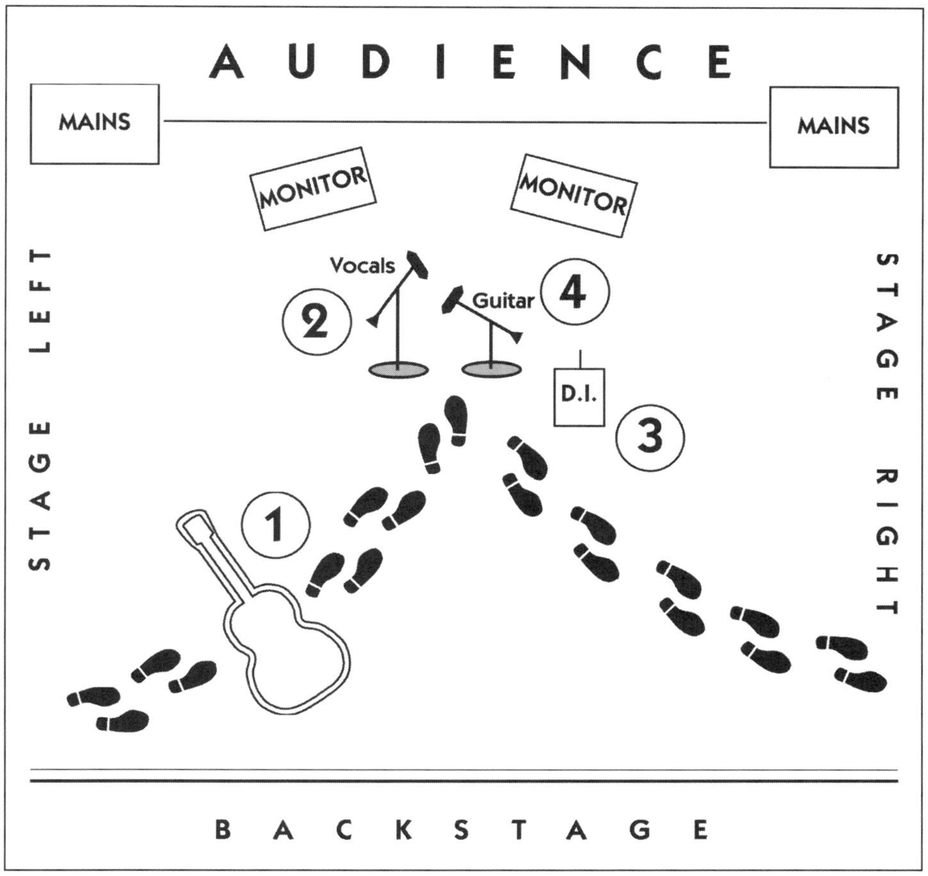

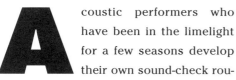

Acoustic performers who have been in the limelight for a few seasons develop their own sound-check routine. Some start by listening to their voice in the monitors, others with the guitar in the mains. The important thing is to be consistent and develop a method that helps you to identify and correct problems before moving on to something else that depends on prior steps. You must understand your process so that you can direct it from the stage proactively. When you have the ear of sympathetic sound technicians that you trust, use them as a sounding board to check the logic of your procedure. This will help fine-tune your sound-check routine so that you can confidently get through situations where time is short or the sound equipment (or technician) is marginal. The following routine is based on my own philosophy and experience, and I believe it can generate consistent results.

The first few minutes of your sound check will set the tone for the rest of the gig. Starting a dialogue with your sound operator *du jour* is important because your sound is literally in their hands. Learn his or her name first, because you'll need it every time you want the sound system adjusted. Using the sound person's name at the beginning of each request helps things go more smoothly. The operative word is *request.* Starting your requests with phrases like "Bob, would it be possible . . ." makes it easier for your technician to comply. Remember, egos are like noses: everyone has one and they all smell. Equally important is "thank you." All this may seem like common sense, but remember that the way performers adjust their sound system is by using another's hands. It's not just the sound equipment you're managing, but also its operator.

SETTING UP THE GEAR

Start by talking about your equipment requirements so that the needed mics, stands, or direct boxes can be located, plugged in, and readied. If there is another performer opening for you, ask if you can use separate channels in the mixing board so that adjustments made at sound check will be preserved until your set (and you can play together). This is a good time to get your instrument out and prepare it and any accessories you brought along. While you're doing this, you can answer questions about specific needs you have, such as a stool or electrical power on stage (your own power strip and extension cord can be lifesavers). The time to change batteries or strings is before you start your sound check, so your sound doesn't change after you check. Any problems that require a Radio Shack or music store solution must be found before the store closes. Plug in your guitar and make sure it works. Don't mess with levels yet. Simply make sure your equipment won't keep you from getting through the show.

Permanent sound systems have the advantage of needing little preparation other than plugging cables into the inputs. Systems brought in by a sound company, on the other hand, can require hours of getting the big chunks in place and running wires before they are ready. Ask the technician how soon he will be ready for you. This question shows that you are aware of your sound tech's needs and will stay out of the way until then. Let him or her know how much time you need and be aware of how your check fits into the schedule of other events, such as a dinner break, doors opening, or other performers' sound checks. Never jump in front of the mic until you know that it's ready.

Adjust the mic stands so that their height, angles, and locations allow you to perform comfortably. If another performer is going on before you, unplugging your vocal mic after sound check and putting the mic and stand off to the side is the easiest way to make sure it will be set the way you want when you come on stage. A second mic and stand can be used for the other performer(s). Bringing your own vocal mic makes it easier for your tech to comply with this request. If you are using separate channels, it can just be set to the side and turned off, awaiting your return for your set.

ADVICE FROM TOP SOUNDMEN

RICHARD BATTAGLIA (BELA FLECK)

I come from the school of making the best of the situation. You have an acoustic instrument, the guitar, on a stage with several other instruments, trying to project to an audience of 250–10,000 folks. How do you get the most representative sound? It's a combination of pickup and mic. The big problem in miking an instrument on stage is trying to get it up in the monitors so each musician can hear the guitar, then getting it up loud in the house speakers. It's a very difficult thing to do. So the pickup and mic approach gives you a much better chance of achieving your goals.

The next step would be ear monitors. This situation is a luxury but can produce great results. I have just recently had the opportunity to mix some of the greatest bluegrass musicians on a four-week tour. We performed to audiences of 500–6,000 folks, and it worked every time. All the guys were using in-ear monitors: Béla Fleck on banjo, Sam Bush on mandolin, Jerry Douglas on Dobro, Stuart Duncan and Gabe Witcher on fiddle, Mark Schatz on bass, and Bryan Sutton on guitar. We were able to use high-quality mics (AKG 452s for the guitars) on all the instruments, no pickups, except the bass. There were no monitors on stage, so the microphones were only picking up each instrument and the sound of the stage. It was a great success. We carried our own monitor mix board, so every night started where the last night left off. Each guy could continue to fine-tune the mix they were hearing. This also allowed the band to walk out on stage without a sound check and hit it with the confidence that they were going to hear all the other guys right off the bat!

PAUL KNIGHT

What I do requires a lot of EQing the PA. That is probably 90 percent of it, no matter what microphone you use. In a classical setting, some jazz settings, and a solo performance setting, everything is much easier. But when you're in a group setting and the guitar player is the lead player, then come the problems, because the guitar is usually one of the quieter of the instruments. That's where EQ of the monitor is just prime. What I've started to do now is to insert a parametric EQ on the guitar channel. I'll go in there, maybe around 160 or 200K, and get a little scoop out of it, so that when the

MAINS, THEN MONITORS

Begin your sound check with your voice in the mains. Seasoned operators may already have the vocal mic ready and just need to turn it on, but it may take unfamiliar techs a few minutes of fiddling with the knobs. Using your voice continuously helps them to adjust your vocal. You've already spent some time talking to your sound operator, so he or she should have some idea what your speaking voice is like and can get the tone of your voice in the mains to sound natural. Speak in your normal voice, but try to be enthusiastic and humorous for a few minutes, if only to entertain yourself, again using your operator's name. Then sing a verse of a song to warm up and show the sound person the difference between your singing and speaking voice. Ask to start without reverb or other effects. If you hear the reverb come into the mains, ask the sound tech to wait on that until last.

Only after each input is working well in the main speakers should you adjust it in the monitors. The *gain* knob at the top of each channel is more likely to be set correctly after the operator has first heard that channel in the mains. Many operators like to operate their faders at a "nominal" position, around 0 dB. Adjusting the mains first allows operators to get the fader to the nominal position by adjusting the gain knob if they mix that way, and many do. If the monitors are adjusted before the gain has been set, the monitor level will go up or down with any changes to the overall channel gain. This "mains first"

soundhole gets into the mic the guitarist is getting the extra oomph but I can take out the muddiness.

I've been using AKG 535s on everything, partially because of the cost consideration. I have ten of them, and if I do a bluegrass festival they're on every voice and every instrument, so I EQ the system with that mic in mind.

A mistake that's commonly made is when musicians listen to the monitor with the house sound off, and they get the soundman to make the monitor sound really beautiful to them. Then when I turn on the house speakers, the first thing I hear is, "Are the monitors off?" It's a huge mistake. When I tell musicians to listen to the monitors, the first thing I want to know is, "Can you hear yourself? Are you loud enough, and clear enough?" I only correct what really sticks out—feedback or just really harsh, horrible tones. Then if it sounds kind of midrangey, it's probably right, because when you bring the house speakers up you'll get your lows and a lot of high frequencies from there.

LARRY CUMINGS (DAVID GRISMAN QUINTET)

I have two mics [on DGQ guitarist Enrique Coria], a Neumann KM 85 and a Shure SM81, and I use a T-Bar with one mic stand. The 81 has a bass roll-off switch, and I have it rolled off all the way. The mics make a V, pointing toward each other at a 45-degree angle. I do this for two reasons. One is for the phase properties that will help the gain for the guitar through the monitor, and the second reason is to have a larger sounding guitar.

I carry with me a few CDs that I produced and engineered, and I listen to them through the PA so I know what it should sound like. I don't use any EQ on David's mandolin microphone, so his microphone sets the standard for the PA. I tune everything around his mic being flat. Typically, I've got to take a lot of bottom end out on the guitar. The consoles I'm using are Yamaha 4000s, and they have a sweepable high-pass filter. I focus on about 200 cycles and sharpen the Q and pull that out. That gets rid of a lot of that boominess. I'm not a guy that adds EQ—I subtract it. If something doesn't sound right, I take it out.

For festivals, where it's act after act with no sound check, I pretty much just use 57s and 58s—Betas mainly—so that the monitor engineer has his system tuned to those mics. I find that I can get a really good sound with those types of mics in a festival situation.

sequence also allows the performer to hear the true level on stage by listening first to just the mains and then to the wedges in combination with sound going out to the room.

Before you even try listening to the monitors, make sure they're aiming right over your shoulders and past your ears, rather than at the mic, guitar, or ceiling. Move the mic stand or the monitors until the angles are right. Next, listen carefully to your voice in the monitors. Encourage your operator to come up on stage, listen to what you hear, and even talk into your mic for comparison. Many operators assume the monitors are OK as long as they're not feeding back and tend to overuse the graphic EQ, giving the monitors a thin or muffled sound. Your voice should sound full, natural, and balanced with the room's sound. Don't move on to checking your guitar until you are reasonably happy with how your voice sounds. Graphic equalizers have about 30 sliders, so there are many possible settings, many of which will sound bad. Often the best settings are mostly flat, with only the worst frequencies cut. This process always takes more time than you'd like and requires patience. Never let the operator "ring out" the feedback in the monitors while you are standing in front of them, because those loud squeals can be damaging to your ears. Leave the stage immediately and come back after the squeaking stops.

Producer-like comments, such as "Sounds a little boxy (bright, thin, muffled, etc.); what do you think, Bob?" helps establish a dialogue and a common audio vocabulary with the sound person. By accompanying verbal requests to raise or lower levels with hand motions, you establish signals that can be used later, during your performance, without talking. Succinct directions can be given with a three-part motion. Pointing to your mouth, then pointing toward the ceiling is easily interpreted as "more vocal." Following this with thumb and forefinger an inch apart means "a little bit." Acknowledging correct adjustments with a stage smile and a nod of the head completes the transaction, paving the way for future adjustments and encouraging your technician to keep an eye on you.

MICS VS. PICKUPS

Those of you who work without a pickup will find it harder to get a meaningful guitar volume in the monitor before feedback starts, particularly if the mic is on a stand instead of mounted on or in the guitar. Because the floor monitor's distance to the guitar mic is about half the distance to the vocal mic, it feeds back at a much lower level and becomes the limiting factor on how loud the monitors can get, unless you get accustomed to less guitar in the monitors.

One strategy for the pickup-less guitarist is to stand very still so that the mic stays close to the instrument. Sitting on a stool rather than a chair offers a height advantage that helps the feedback situation a little. If you sit on a chair, moving back from the monitors will help a little, but you may then need to prop up the wedges. Sitting, of course, is not the best way to sing. Ultimately you will end up with some kind of pickup if you want the guitar in the monitors at a significant level. It's wise to spend the extra money on a good one.

Having a pickup in an acoustic guitar offers the benefit of a sound source that is immune to feedback compared to a microphone. Because it is part of the guitar, its sound won't change as you move around. When using a guitar mic as well, having only the pickup in the monitors greatly reduces feedback problems. Start by getting a rough level on the guitar's pickup, mains first and then monitors. As soon as you and your sound tech can hear it clearly, adjust any preamp tone controls you have for your guitar, as they affect what is heard both on stage and in the audience. After you are satisfied with the sound of the guitar in the monitors, help the sound engineer by talking to him about the sound of your pickup while you play several different styles. The mixing board's tone controls can be used to further adjust the pickup in the main speakers, but they will not affect the pickup's monitor send. Explain how you want the guitar to sound, but remember that while you are on stage listening to monitors it may be difficult to hear changes being made in the mains.

Some pickups do not sound completely natural, and using a microphone to supplement the guitar sound in the main speakers helps. Some players ask for 40 percent pickup and 60 percent microphone, but the combination varies for different styles of playing. The idea is to combine the best parts of both inputs to create a good composite guitar sound. Some pickups have a brittle, harsh top end, and by rolling off the highs and using a guitar mic to add highs to the mains, a better sound can be achieved. The guitar mic in the mains may be less stable in the lower frequencies, especially if you move around while you play. Using the pickup more for lows and the mic more for highs usually provides a workable blend.

Discussing all this with your sound person ("It's Bob, right?") will help him focus on what he's adjusting. You can mix your own sound a little by leaning the guitar toward the mic as you switch from strumming to picking, or between lyrics. Some operators may be skilled enough to turn your guitar up and down a little with different playing styles, but many will need to be reminded to do this during sound check. There's no guarantee they'll remember during your set, but this is the time to begin an attempt. One way to mix yourself is to have an A-B switcher and use two direct boxes, setting one channel for picking and the other for strumming.

EFFECTS

Add in a little reverb last. Effects are like the sauce or spices in a good meal—they should enhance but not overpower. Settings of 2 to 3 seconds are nice, with longer settings for ballads and shorter ones for up-tempo pieces. One rule of thumb is to turn the reverb up to where you can just hear it and then go back down a touch. Cutting the reverb's EQ a little helps it blend it in with the mains. Putting a little reverb on the guitar pickup can help it sound less amplified, but too much will make it distant and indistinct. Too much on your voice makes it harder to understand the lyrics and sounds funny when you talk between songs. Generally, reverb in the monitors will not help much and can fool you about how you really sound. Try turning the monitors down a bit instead and listen more to the mains.

CHECK . . . CHECK

OK, time for a quick review. First your voice in the mains, then in the monitors as you patiently adjust the EQ. Next, deal with the guitar pickup, adjusting first your preamp's EQ then the board's EQ. Then add the guitar mic in the mains and a dash of reverb. Many performers who have been doing this for years have gotten this routine down to a few minutes. All this advice changes in festival situations with multiple performers sharing the stage, where you simply get a guitar level in the monitors and then perform. With time, you'll develop a regular dialogue for your sound-check routine, complete with jokes ("It was in tune when I bought it") that will help you know in advance what kind of night it's going to be. Hey, how many bluegrass musicians does it take to change a light bulb? Five. One for the bulb and four to discuss how much better it was before it was electric.

NOTCHING OUT FEEDBACK

Sometimes during a sound check you will notice that a particular note on the guitar is causing the monitors to growl in a threatening manner. Isolating the specific frequency of the offending note can often help a savvy sound tech contour or notch the monitor EQ to ameliorate the problem. It's handy to know the frequencies of your open strings, and you can interpolate from there to find the frequencies of frets between the open notes. Here are the approximate open-string frequencies in standard tuning:

E	83 Hz
A	110 Hz
D	147 Hz
G	196 Hz
B	247 Hz
E	330 Hz

If your guitar howls in the monitors every time you hit an open D, for example, you might suggest to the sound person that you've got a hot spot right around 150 Hz and maybe he or she should try easing back that frequency in the monitor EQ. This doesn't always do the trick, but having a sense of the open-string frequencies can often speed up the sound-check process when feedback is a problem, and it can be a life saver when you are doing your own sound.

—Paul Kotapish

Getting the Best Guitar Sound on Stage

Scott Nygaard

Scott Nygaard at the Rocky Mountain Folks Festival.

There is a wealth of information available to the acoustic musician concerning the technical mysteries of PA systems—what each component does, how the pieces go together, what you should look for when purchasing, what is essential, which components are a luxury or necessary only for a certain style of music, and so on. Most of this information is written by sound reinforcement engineers, not musicians. This makes sense (owner's manuals for automobiles are written by mechanics, not drivers), but some direction from the other side of the mic stand may be just as helpful.

Not that there isn't plenty of advice coming from this quarter. Anyone willing to brave the raging waters of the Internet will find endless debates, many contentious and personality-driven, on questions like whether to use microphones or pickups, both, or in extreme cases, neither. But in the megabyte realm it is often difficult to separate information from polemics. So, for those of you who have acquired some basic information about sound reinforcement (for instance, you are able to correctly answer the question, "What are those boxes on the floor in front of the performers?"), here is some real-world advice and opinion gleaned from years of standing behind a microphone saying, "Test . . . test. Is this thing on?"

SOUND TECH ETIQUETTE

Always treat the sound engineer with respect. The first thing to remember is that everyone has an opinion about the way the music sounds, but there is only one person whose hands rest on the knobs, so you'd better make sure that person is on your side. Do all you can to avoid alienating or angering your sound engineer, even if he or she is currently making you sound like a hyena in heat.

Give the sound engineer time to figure out how to make the sound work. Most musicians' natural inclination is to begin giving advice about how to alter and color the sound as soon as their microphone is turned on—as if the engineer is deaf or in another room and can't hear what everyone else is hearing. Every combination of room, equipment, and musician is different, and if you're using a good PA with a fair amount of equalization, then the engineer often just needs to hear you play for awhile. This may seem obvious, but I've seen many professional musicians with years of experience, who don't understand that when the sound starts changing dramatically—often negatively—during sound check, the engineer is not trying to annoy the performer, but is experimenting with different EQ possibilities. For instance, oftentimes there is a peak or valley in the signal that is negatively affecting the tone of an instrument. In order to zero in on this particular frequency, the engineer will boost the EQ in the general range that is causing the problem, then sweep through that range, boosting different frequencies. Let the engineer do what needs to be done; then, when he or she seems satisfied, you can make comments about the sound. He or she will be much more willing to take your advice at this point, as it will appear that you know a little about sound reinforcement yourself and have actually been on a stage before.

Establish a system for your sound checks. I usually try to check the guitar first. This is helpful because the acoustic guitar's output is often considerably less than other instruments in a band and will allow the gain and overall levels to be set accordingly. If the gain is set to the loudest instrument in the bunch, it may be necessary to turn the guitar up to 11 (an option available only to members of bands that travel with their own hairdressers) to make it loud enough. Of course, if you're going to check the guitar first, you should be ready first: in tune, plugged in if it's appropriate, and with the mic stands adjusted accordingly. The disadvantage with checking the guitar first is that sometimes, after you have the guitar where you want it, there will be a problem with some other aspect of the PA that will cause the engineer to radically change the EQ of the entire system, potentially ruining the sound of the guitar. In order to avoid this, try checking a vocal next. You can usually tell from the sound of the vocal if the system's EQ is completely out of whack. If the overall EQ does need adjusting, at least you've discovered the problem before you get to the end of a long sound check and the audience is beating down the doors.

WHAT'S THE BUZZ?

Q *My soundhole pickup creates a buzz on some PA systems and not on others. What could be the source of the buzz, and how can I fix it?*

A Soundhole pickups magnetically induct the vibrations of metal strings, and—like those on many electric guitars—they tend to be single-pole pickups. Double-pole pickups, called humbuckers, are found on some electrics and are designed to cancel out interference. Soundhole pickups give acoustic guitars higher resistance to feedback, along with that hollow-body electric sound. Better-made models, such as the Sunrise, have improved frequency response and can sound quite good. The disadvantage can be the accompanying buzz that is often due to unbalanced or unshielded cables.

The fact that you experience this buzz on some systems and not others indicates that the cause of trouble lies outside of your pickup. Interference is frequently caused by SCR wall dimmers, which are used in some smaller clubs to save the expense of a professional lighting system (although those can also cause interference). One way to verify that the lights are the source of the buzz is to turn them up and then off while listening, but this doesn't present a solution, since performing in the dark is usually not an option.

Other buzzes are caused by trying to run an unbalanced signal over too great a distance to a mixer's quarter-inch jack input. Most soundhole pickups terminate in a quarter-inch plug. The low-level, high-impedance, unbalanced signal that comes out of this plug can only run a couple of dozen feet before it becomes susceptible to interference. Plugging into a direct box, or DI, on stage converts it into a low-impedance, balanced signal that can be fed into the mixer with a three-pin XLR mic cable, just like a microphone. Direct boxes also have a switch on them that lifts the ground on the XLR, which can block interference as the signal travels down the cable to the mixing board.

—Mark Frink

DAVID TANENBAUM ON MIKING A CLASSICAL GUITAR

I find the best placement to be low, and by the bottom (biggest) bout of the guitar, in other words to the right of the bridge on the treble side. When working as a soloist with orchestras, I think it's important to have a source by the player, so you don't see the guitarist in one place and the sound coming from speakers somewhere else. I usually combine an amp near me with the house system, and I always insist that there be monitors behind the orchestra, one on each side, so they can hear the guitar player. Many orchestras comment on how helpful that is.

MIC TECHNIQUES

There are many ways to mic a guitar and at least three times as many opinions as there are successful methods. Probably the most common method is to point the microphone at the end of the fingerboard. For years the mantra has been "just not in the soundhole," particularly if you're playing a dreadnought. Lately I've discovered that pointing the microphone directly into the top of the soundhole can be a great idea (I hear legions of sound engineers groaning as I write this). The gain increase is significant, and if you have a mixing board with a bass roll-off at the desired frequency, or a microphone with minimal bass response, you can get a great sound this way. It won't always work. Sometimes it is not possible to roll off enough bass, or the bass EQ on the board is set at the wrong frequency, but I always give it a try. If you have no time to do a proper sound check—for example, festivals with no time between acts—be sure to alert the sound engineer that you intend to point the mic into the soundhole. But don't persist for too long. If after the first couple of songs your guitar is still sounding like a 747 taking off, back off and give your band members a break.

Some sound engineers will insist that they know better about microphone placement than you do. Sometimes they do, sometimes they don't. You may be able to learn a new technique by listening to their advice, but sometimes they are just completely off track. I can remember a number of people trying to get me to point the microphone at a spot just below the bridge. This might work for fingerstyle players with very little right-hand movement, but, in my case, the sound of my arm crashing into the mic every time I strummed a chord was just too distracting.

WORKING THE MIC

Treat the microphone as if it's a small child: know where it is at all times. In a band situation it is necessary to work the microphone as a singer would. Back off (six to 12 inches) when you're playing strongly or don't need to be heard so clearly (playing rhythm), then get right on the microphone when you're playing a solo or fill—or something quieter than normal, such as switching to playing with your fingers after a long period of pick-aided thrashing. Working the microphone like this can often make a band look like a bunch of stick figures glued to the stage and is one reason people use pickups—so that they can move around while they are playing and still be heard. I've found that it *is* possible to dance your dance and still work the mic effectively. Just imagine that a foot-long string is tied from the microphone to the soundhole. Then move—dance, bob, weave, gyrate, nod thoughtfully—accordingly.

Supplying your own microphone can be helpful if you've found one that sounds particularly good on your guitar, but if its sound is radically different from the sound of the other mics you're using, it may make things more difficult. Tossing a high-quality condenser microphone into a den of off-brand dynamic mics is not a pretty sound. In addition, the sound engineer may know how to get a good sound using the equipment he or she is used to working with but be unfamiliar with the particular characteristics of your microphone. The microphone is just one piece in the whole chain. The amplifiers, mixing board, outboard effects, EQ, and speakers have as much to do with the sound of the PA as an individual microphone.

PICKUPS

My favorite way to amplify an acoustic guitar for the stage is to use a microphone, but in many situations some form of pickup is almost a necessity. A pickup will never make your guitar sound the way you hear it acoustically, but if you are trying to get a "natural" sound and are forced by circumstances to use a pickup, some adjustment to your mind-set may be wise. Imagine that your guitar with pickup installed is a completely different instrument, one that may not have your ideal acoustic sound, but one whose tone can nevertheless be quite pleasing and more suited to the situation, i.e., louder.

Adding a preamp and some form of EQ to the signal path is the first step toward a good pickup sound. Never plug a piezo-type pickup directly into the board (at least not while I'm in the area, please). Everything in the signal path is critical. Use a high-quality, shielded cable that goes directly to your preamp and then add in whatever EQ and effects you desire. Adding a lot of effects may make the signal deteriorate, so try to find the one or two things that improve your sound the most and just use those. One frequent error when using a small (three- to six-band) graphic EQ is cutting every frequency to some degree—which is effectively just turning the volume down. Use the EQ judiciously and be just as willing to boost frequencies as cut them. Check any nine-volt batteries in your effects and preamp regularly. When batteries go dead, they often don't just shut off—a problem in itself—but can distort the signal as they near the end of their life.

One problem with pickups is a lack of dynamic range, which is exacerbated by the fact that some pickups sound worse when you're in string-thrashing mode. Adding a volume pedal or working an external microphone—used in addition to the pickup—can help solve this problem, but keeping your foot (and eyes) glued to a volume pedal can be restricting. It is possible to rig a system of setting two volumes by using an on/off–style foot switch in conjunction with an effects unit. Set the effects output gain so that your guitar signal is louder when the foot switch is on, and then you can give yourself a bit of a boost for solos or fills by simply hitting the switch. You can also contour or color the sound with the addition of the effect. For instance, you may want a rhythm sound that is bright and punchy and a solo sound that is fat and warm.

GROUND HUM

Q *Last time I plugged my acoustic-electric guitar into a PA I got a bad hum that could only be stopped by touching the metal end of my cord. What could be the cause and cure for this ground problem?*

A Grounding hum can be a devilish thing to diagnose, but here are some ideas. Virtually all under-saddle pickups are very high-impedance devices, which are inherently sensitive to hum. First, make sure that the pickup and any wiring going to its preamp are scrupulously shielded and grounded to prevent it from acting like an antenna tuned to 60 hertz noise. Also check to see if your strings are connected to a ground. Sometimes adding a grounding plate under the bridge (which all the strings contact) can stop hum. I've made plates with a thin sheet of brass drilled for the string pegs and a ground wire going to the jack.

You will often find that different electronics in the total system—PA, stage gear, etc.—have different ground references to the AC system. This is why many direct boxes have ground lift switches, and some older amps have ground switches (though these have been supplanted with polarized two-prong or grounded three-prong AC connectors). If you have a ground lift switch anywhere in your system, try flipping it the other way and see if the hum gets better.

Another thing to try is going back to the PA console and plugging directly into the board. This will eliminate the possibility of bad wiring from the stage to the mixer. If the hum goes away when you are plugged in directly, then it's probably a club wiring problem. PA system wiring takes a lot of abuse and should be maintained constantly. Cables get crunched, plugs get reversed, amps blow up, parts go bad, and hum just happens.

—Rick Turner

SHOW TIME

Doubtless there are many more tips like these available from those who have stumbled upon them, as I have, from experience. But everyone's musical situation and taste is different. You may have to do most of your own stumbling. Be willing to take advice (along with the proverbial grain of salt) and be willing to challenge received wisdom. Technology changes quickly, and standard approaches to sound reinforcement may be very different in the space of just a few years. Oh, and one last piece of advice. Don't continue the sound check into the performance. One of the quickest ways to drive the audience out into the cool night air is to keep up a running conversation with the sound engineer while you're performing. Just accept the fact that this is how you're going to sound and get on with it. As a friend of mine once said: When you're done, remember to stop.

How to Get Good Sound at the Last Minute

Rick Turner

"What do you mean, no sound check?"

Sound familiar? All too often, musicians have to rush on stage with little or no sound check. Even when a sound check is possible, it is usually under far different circumstances than the actual performance. Room acoustics change with the addition of people, ambient noise goes up, and the pressure of live performance affects the judgment of both performer and sound mixer. So how do you handle it? Here are some suggestions from both sides of the footlights; I've performed and mixed in many less-than-ideal situations.

There are both physical and psychological components to dealing with sound systems and the people using them. Amplifying acoustic instruments is tricky at best, and mixing live acoustic sound is the true test of a sound mixer. There is always the tendency to push a system very close to the threshold of feedback when amplifying acoustic music, and that seems particularly true under the pressure of "no sound check" situations.

Both performers and mixers have egos to consider. There is nothing a mixer hates more than being told what to do, and there is nothing a performer hates more than a poor mix. Can the twain e'er meet? Usually, with a little mutual cooperation they can.

No matter whether small club or large hall, the path to acceptable (maybe even great!) sound starts with communication. Sound mixers are often a bit defensive about their job; they get blamed for every bit of feedback, inaudibility, or sonic muddiness. No musician likes giving up artistic control of their sound to a total stranger who may or may not be qualified; you certainly wouldn't do that in the studio. Too often, mixers in small clubs have the job by default.

Yet here you are, doing a guest set at Club X, and you suspect that the sound person has never mixed anything more subtle than an Iron Maiden clone band! Most important, you need to establish a positive attitude. A mixer who doesn't like you will destroy you. Try to make his job as easy as possible; don't cop an attitude of, "I'm the artist, my job is just to perform. Your job is to mix my set perfectly."

STAGE PLOTS

Give the mixer a stage plot showing musicians' positions, mic requirements for vocals and instruments, and direct plug-ins. If possible, give him a set list that notes any instrument changes, an idea of the relative levels desired for instruments, and even what instrumental breaks to look out for. If there is a selection of different mics, know what works best for you. Many musicians carry their own mics, but you should check first with the sound person before you change mics on stage. If you use a condenser mic that requires phantom power, for instance, it may not be compatible with the system you are playing through, or phantom power may only be available on certain channels.

One of the most common problems with "instant mixing" is confusion regarding mic or direct channel assignment. "Is the vocalist's guitar on line 1 or 4? Did you just switch mics? I thought he plugged into line 6, but there's nothing there. . . . Oops, that's the backup singer's mic!" Yes, it happens, and all the time, even on big tours when everything is supposed to be the same every night. Causes can be operator inexperience, channel reassignment because of partial equipment failure, last-minute decisions regarding mic types, and mostly lack of communication between stage and mixer.

Try to coordinate a routine of going through each mic or direct feed before you start your set to confirm that channel assignments are what they are supposed to be. This takes cooperation of all band members; each should be quiet while the others' channels are being confirmed. Each channel should be soloed briefly to check assignment and rough EQ. This gives the mixer a chance to get everything sorted out. Ask the mixer to write down final channel assignments so that if you have a friend help mix there won't be any confusion. It's better to take a couple of minutes getting it right at the beginning of the set than to be constantly pleading or cursing during the set. There's nothing like a battle between musician and sound person to ruin a set.

Guitarist and electronics expert Rick Turner.

ONE MIX

Under "no sound check" conditions, I find it best to have the same mix in both house and monitor speakers. In that way, performers have a good idea of what the audience is hearing and can make adjustments and suggestions to the mixer. Most PA consoles have separate monitor mix capability, and separate mixers are often appropriate under ideal conditions. For most clubs and in most last-minute situations, however, separate mixes for house and stage just make everything more confusing. You are going to be fortunate to get just one good mix; don't try for two.

YOUR GEAR

If you use a direct feed from your instrument, carry a couple of good cables of different lengths to match stage conditions. I find having an eight-foot and a 20-foot cable covers all situations. You might consider carrying your own direct box to match quarter-inch unbalanced connectors to three-pin XLR connector balanced lines. If you use outboard gear, try to have it configured for minimum setup time. Know that all your gear works. If there is a problem with anything on your channel, the sound person will first blame your equipment, right or wrong.

If you have EQ in your system, use it to get your basic instrument sound using headphones, and then mark all knob positions. Avoid changing those settings on stage; they establish your basic sound. Any further EQ should be to correct system or house irregularities, not the sound of the instrument. Otherwise you and the sound person are likely to get into counteracting each others' EQing, ultimately making the sound worse and worse. Use as little EQ as possible; it introduces phase irregularities that destroy sonic detail.

VOLUME

I find that it is always better to err on the side of too little overall volume at the start of a set than too much. With the mix a bit on the soft side, there is a better chance of getting a good balance between instruments and vocals without running into feedback. Once you achieve a working balance, then the master volume can be slowly raised to the desired level. Regarding volume: I find that all too many sound people are attuned to rock sound pressure levels. They want your D-18 to sound like a Les Paul! Try gently suggesting that you might sound better with the overall level 3 or 4 decibels softer than normal for starters. Volume is no substitute for musical intensity; the excesses of rock volume need not be extended to acoustic music.

Perhaps the best thing you can do under any circumstances is have a friend at the gig who knows your music and who can communicate effectively with the sound person. The mixer may not like being told what to do, but tell him that your friend knows your music well and would like to help get the right balance. The mixer may wind up being more cooperative than you think.

While the lack of a sound check is certainly a handicap, it need not ruin your night if you are prepared and cooperative. Note, too, that all these suggestions for dealing with "no sound check" situations also apply to those dream gigs where you have the best equipment in the world and a two-hour sound check. Preparation and a good attitude are the main components of a great gig.

THANK YOU FOR PURCHASING ONE OF *Acoustic Guitar* MAGAZINE'S MUSIC BOOKS

We hope you enjoy learning and playing the music provided in this book. This and material just like it has appeared in the pages of *Acoustic Guitar* Magazine.

3 FREE ISSUES!

YES! I'll take three free issues of *Acoustic Guitar* Magazine, along with a money-saving introductory subscription of 12 monthly issues for just $23.95. That's 15 issues in all, filled with exclusive "Private Lessons," artist profiles, and great advice on guitars and gear. I save $50.30 off the retail price, and I may cancel at any time, for any reason, and receive a full refund.

Name ______________________________ AGBK00

Address ______________________________

City __________ State __________ Zip __________ Country __________

Phone __________ E-mail __________

☐ Payment enclosed ☐ Bill me later.

Please allow 4–6 weeks for delivery of your first issue. Add $15 for Canada/Pan Am; $30 elsewhere outside the U.S. Pay in U.S. funds on U.S. bank. Visa/MasterCard/American Express accepted.

THANK YOU FOR PURCHASING ONE OF *Acoustic Guitar* MAGAZINE'S MUSIC BOOKS

We hope you enjoy learning and playing the music provided in this book. This and material just like it has appeared in the pages of *Acoustic Guitar* Magazine.

3 FREE ISSUES!

YES! I'll take three free issues of *Acoustic Guitar* Magazine, along with a money-saving introductory subscription of 12 monthly issues for just $23.95. That's 15 issues in all, filled with exclusive "Private Lessons," artist profiles, and great advice on guitars and gear. I save $50.30 off the retail price, and I may cancel at any time, for any reason, and receive a full refund.

Name ______________________________ AGBK00

Address ______________________________

City __________ State __________ Zip __________ Country __________

Phone __________ E-mail __________

☐ Payment enclosed ☐ Bill me later.

Please allow 4–6 weeks for delivery of your first issue. Add $15 for Canada/Pan Am; $30 elsewhere outside the U.S. Pay in U.S. funds on U.S. bank. Visa/MasterCard/American Express accepted.

FREE Issue Offer!
See Reverse for
Details!

NO POSTAGE
NECESSARY IF
MAILED
IN THE UNITED
STATES

BUSINESS REPLY MAIL
FIRST CLASS MAIL PERMIT NO. 99020 ESCONDIDO CA

Postage will be paid by addressee

ACOUSTIC
GUITAR

PO Box 469120
Escondido, CA 92046-9570

A Complete Glossary of Amplification Lingo

Rick Turner

AMPLIFIER A device for making small electrical signals bigger. The term often refers to a self-contained "combo amp"—an electro-mechanical device combining a preamp, amplifier, and loudspeaker that usually includes some kinds of tone-shaping circuitry. There are a growing number of combo amps on the market specifically designed for amplifying acoustic guitars.

BUFFER A preamplifier designed to isolate the source from the next stage of amplification. Buffer amps have high input impedances and low output impedances and can also feature some gain- or signal-boosting capability. Buffers are required with piezo crystal or piezo polymer pickups, and several manufacturers, such as Fishman, EMG, Highlander, and Baggs, sell buffer/pickup packages with the buffer designed specifically to go with the pickup. Don't believe the "no buffer necessary" hype from some piezo pickup makers.

CARDIOID MIC A microphone designed to be more sensitive in one direction than in others; a directional mic. Cardioid mics are used more often than other types of mics on stage because they make it easier to isolate one voice or instrument from the others for mixing. Examples include Shure SM57s and SM58s.

CHORUS An electronic device that splits a signal, mildly shifts the pitch and timing of one part, then mixes it back in with the original signal. The effect approximates the sound of several people playing the same part at the same time.

COMPRESSOR A processor that "squeezes" the dynamic range of the signal by limiting peaks and bringing up the level of soft passages. A limiter can be used to fatten a sound or give it more apparent sustain. Too much compression can make the music sound flat (kind of like FM radio), but the Beatles used tons of compression on their acoustic guitar recordings to great effect.

CONDENSER MIC A microphone in which an electrically charged diaphragm moves with sound waves while an oppositely charged back plate stays stationary. Because the diaphragms of condenser mics can be made very lightweight, their frequency response can be very good. An example is the Neumann mic, considered by many to be the ultimate mic for recording voice and acoustic instruments.

CONTACT PICKUPS Sometimes called soundboard transducers, contact pickups are most often piezoelectric accelerometers (acceleration monitors). They put out an electrical signal that is analogous to the mechanical vibrations occurring where they are placed. Classic examples include the Barcus-Berry Hot Dot, the FRAP, and all the piezo transducers based on Radio Shack products.

CONTOURING Using an equalizer to shape the frequency response of a signal or sound system.

DI The British term now common in the U.S. for "directly injecting" a pickup signal into a recording or PA console, thus bypassing amplifiers, speakers, and mics. Excellent for getting a clear tone from an electric bass. Many home recordists DI acoustic guitars with pickups to gain better isolation than they can get with mics.

DIAPHRAGM The microphone's equivalent of an eardrum. The diaphragm vibrates with sound and then transforms that acoustic energy into an electrical signal that can be amplified.

DIGITAL DELAY Abbreviated as DDL. A signal processor in which analog signals are converted into a stream of digital information that can be delayed and mixed to create echo-like sounds. Digital delay is usually included with other sonic colorings in multi-effects processors.

DIRECT BOX A device used to buffer or isolate guitar and bass signals so they can be run through a DI. Many of the direct boxes designed for electric guitars and basses do not have a sufficiently high input impedance for interface with piezo pickups. Direct boxes can either be passive, using transformers, or active, using tube or transistor-based circuitry.

DYNAMIC MIC A mic that works like a backward loudspeaker. The diaphragm is attached to a small coil of very fine wire, which is surrounded by a magnetic field. When the diaphragm and coil vibrate with sound waves, a small electrical signal is generated in the coil, which can be amplified through a mic preamp and other devices. The Shure SM57 and SM58, two of the most common mics used in clubs and studios, are dynamic mics. Dynamic mics are noted for being tough; the mic you can drive a nail with is probably a dynamic.

EFFECTS LOOP A set of jacks on an amp or preamp that allows a signal to be sent out, modified, and brought back through the main unit. The advantage of an effects loop is that it is buffered on the output and input; the impedance level is predictable, and the volume of the modified signal can be controlled in the main amp or preamp.

EQUALIZATION/EQ Electronic means of shaping frequency response. You can think of EQ as sophisticated tone-control circuitry. EQ was originally used to correct the unequal frequency response of old PAs and recording gear.

EXTERNAL MIC Generally refers to the good old mic you stand in front of on stage as opposed to the mic you install in your guitar. There are now some bracket devices for mounting an external mic on your guitar.

FEEDBACK Yowl, howl, feedback by any name is the sonic nemesis of the performer. It happens when amplification goes out of control and the amplified sound itself is recirculating and becoming further amplified. The sonic equivalent of Chernobyl—audio meltdown. *Ringing* is the precursor to feedback; the term refers to a barely controlled resonance just shy of feedback.

FLOATING PICKUP A magnetic pickup mounted to the end of the fingerboard on a guitar or to some other nonvibrating part of a musical instrument. Floating pickups are sometimes used on archtop acoustic guitars, because other pickups might interfere or change the vibration pattern of their tops. The Gibson Johnny Smith pickup is a classic floater.

GRAPHIC EQUALIZER An equalizer that uses sliding potentiometers (slide pots) to control the level of the signal in various frequency bands. The name comes from the fact that the knobs form a graphic representation of the frequency contouring. Graphic equalizers are generally either "third octave" or "tenth octave," referring to the width of the audio bands covered.

GROUND Our British counterparts call it earth, and it means the same basic thing: the master reference point for electrical circuits, whether they are power (AC mains) or signal. The reference point is often quite literal; I once co-owned a recording studio where our ground point was a bronze boat propeller buried about five feet in the ground underneath the mixing console. Ground is the point to which all equipment and cable shields are grounded, and in the audio signal path, ground is the zero point of the signal to which positive and negative waveforms are referenced.

HUMBUCKER A type of pickup that uses two coils to cancel magnetically induced hum (EMF). Invented by Seth Lover at Gibson in the 1950s, the humbucker is known for its loud, warm sound.

IMPEDANCE A characteristic of all electronic signals that's related to how easily current can flow at various frequencies; impedance is not the same as signal voltage or current. What you want is low-impedance sources feeding into high-impedance loads; this gives maximum accuracy in signal transfer.

INTERNAL MIC A mic (generally an electret condenser mic) mounted inside an instrument.

JACK Should probably be called jackie, as it is the female half of a pair of connectors (the males are the plugs). Jacks are found as outputs on guitars and as inputs and outputs on just about everything else. There are numerous styles of jacks and plugs; the ones you are most likely to see on musical gear are phone (quarter-inch) jacks, named after their original use by the phone company (when there was only one); RCA jacks, used on stereo gear; XLR jacks (see below); and MIDI jacks.

LIMITER Kind of like a one-sided compressor, a limiter keeps hot signals from overloading the next stage of electronics. Les Paul takes credit for inventing the limiter used in recording studios. He told me he got the idea from watching Mary Ford turn her head while singing loud passages as she watched the recording V.U. meters. She physically limited the input signal to the mic with this technique.

LINE LEVEL The voltage level at which most pro gear sends preamped signals to other devices, such as equalizers, limiters, and compressors.

MAGNETIC PICKUP A pickup that consists of a magnetic structure and one or more coils of very fine wire that transduce the vibration of steel (cored) strings into an analogous electrical signal.

MIDI Musical Instrument Digital Interface, the computer language used in modern synthesizers and signal processors to communicate with other devices.

MINI-MIC Small microphones available at your local mini-mart. Actually, mini-mics were derived from hearing aids and CIA mic-in-the-martini-olive technology. These are generally electret mics, a simpler variation on the condenser mic.

MIXER Used to combine or mix multiple sound signals into a mono, stereo, or other simpler signal to go onto tape, CD, or through a PA system. Also refers to the person who does the mixing, not to be confused with the remixer, the person who doesn't mix live but works on mix-downs of prerecorded mix-ups.

MONITOR Generally refers to a set of speakers that allow performers to hear themselves on stage. Watch for in-ear monitors, the latest thing in stage monitoring; these are like hearing aids for musicians.

"NATURAL" SOUND Often achieved with the most unnatural of means, natural sound is the Holy Grail of most acoustic musicians. To hear it, try listening to truly acoustic music; no, no, not *MTV Unplugged!*

NOTCH FILTER A specialized equalizer that can be tuned to "notch out" particularly annoying frequencies. Often used to kill a feedback frequency.

ON-BOARD/OUTBOARD Generally refers to where pickup buffering and/or EQ stages are located. On-board is in your instrument; outboard is somewhere else, man.

PA Originally referred to *public address system*. Remember "Would Johnny Jones come to the principal's office"? Now the term refers to the sound systems designed for amplifying live music.

PARAMETRIC EQ A type of equalizer that allows continuous control over three parameters: frequency, bandwidth, and amount of boost or cut. While harder to understand than graphic equalizers, parametric EQ is preferred by pro audio engineers for fixing specific sonic problems without affecting other frequencies.

PHANTOM POWER A system wherein DC current used to power on-board electronics or a condenser mic is run up the same cable used to send signal down to a mixer. Used most often in the studio for high-end condenser mics, but also used by Pendulum Audio for powering piezo buffer preamps.

PHASING The relative polarity of two or more signals that contain similar information. In-phase signals add together, while out-of-phase signals tend to cancel. Phasing also applies to loudspeakers.

PICKUP A device that changes the vibrations of a soundboard or strings into an electrical signal.

PIEZOELECTRIC Certain crystals, ceramics, and polymers exhibit the phenomenon of piezoelectricity. Piezo means *pressure* in Greek, and piezo materials directly transform mechanical vibrations into electrical signals.

PLUG *See* jack

POLEPIECES Magnetically conductive elements of a magnetic pickup used to shape the magnetic field. Did I mention that they're magnetic?

PREAMP An electronic device usually designed for matching low-level signals to a power amplifier. EQ and other signal processing is usually done within the preamp stage.

PRESENCE CONTROL A section or knob of an equalizer operating in the upper midrange.

PROCESSOR A signal-modifying device that often combines several effects, such as EQ, chorus, delay, and reverb.

PROXIMITY EFFECT A characteristic of cardioid mics wherein low end is boosted as you get closer to the mic. Proximity effect can make a mic sound overly boomy if you get too close.

RACK-MOUNT Gear that is designed to be mounted in the international standard 19-inch rack. The standard was set by the phone company for its racks upon racks of electrical switches, which routed phone calls in days of old.

REVERB Surf music's sound. Reverb is like echo, but less discreet.

RIBBON MIC A type of microphone in which a very thin conductive ribbon, often aluminum, vibrates in a magnetic field. A small current is induced in the ribbon itself and is then preamped like other types of mic signal.

SIGNAL The word I've used more often than any other in this glossary. In amplification, the signal is the electrical analog of the musical note(s) traveling through the amplification chain.

SINGLE-COIL Generally refers to a magnetic pickup having one coil of magnetic wire. Noted for a certain clarity and focus.

THREE-BAND Refers to equalizers having low-, mid-, and high-frequency controls.

TRANSDUCER Any device that changes mechanical or acoustic energy into an electrical signal or vice versa. Mics, pickups, and loudspeakers are all transducers. The term is often used to refer to accelerometer-style piezo pickups, but it is not exclusive to such pickups.

TRANSIENT RESPONSE How fast a preamp, amplifier, or signal processor responds to an input signal. Related to *slew rate*. Fast is good; slow is bad.

TUBE An electrical device that can amplify low-level signals. Called a *valve* in England because it works like a faucet that controls a large volume of water. Tubes are the oldest technology used for this purpose and are still preferred by many for preamps, direct boxes, and amplifiers. They're made of glass similar to that used in lightbulbs, and boy, do they get hot!

TWEETER A loudspeaker designed specifically for high frequencies. Tweeters usually cover the range from 3,000 or 4,000 cycles (3 to 4 kilohertz) on up to 20 kilohertz. Think Tweetie Bird.

WOOFER A loudspeaker designed to reproduce low frequencies, generally from 20 Hz up to 1 to 3 kilohertz. Midrange drivers are sometimes used to cover the frequencies between 1 and 4 kilohertz.

XLR A type of jack/plug connector most often seen as microphone and pro audio equipment jacks. XLRs are usually seen in their three-pin version, though they are available in up to seven-pin configurations. The most common wiring is that pin one is ground, pin two is "signal low side," and pin three is "signal high side."

Other Titles from String Letter Publishing

All Include Audio CD

Acoustic Guitar Lead and Melody Basics

The experts at *Acoustic Guitar* provide the fundamentals of playing leads in a variety of styles, so players can make a smooth transition from accompanist to soloist. *(64 pp., $14.95, Item #21695492, ISBN 1-890490-19-9)*

Acoustic Guitar Accompaniment Basics

For beginners as well as seasoned players looking to brush up on the basics, this in-depth CD lesson book provides the essentials of acoustic guitar accompaniment utilizing both fingerpicking and flatpicking techniques in a number of roots styles. *(60 pp., $14.95, Item #21695430, ISBN 1-890490-11-3)*

Classical Guitar Answer Book

In this expanded edition of *The Classical Guitar Answer Book,* virtuoso and head of the Juilliard School Guitar Department, Sharon Isbin, answers 50 essential questions about performing, practicing, choosing, and caring for your guitar. An absolute must for every classical guitar player. *(Book only, 84 pp., $14.95, Item #21330443, ISBN 1-890490-08-3)*

Flatpicking Guitar Essentials

If you love bluegrass and folk music, you'll enjoy using this popular guide to learn flatpicking backup styles, melodies, and leads. The outstanding lessons will inspire you to transcribe bluegrass solos, flatpick fiddle tunes, and add power to your solos. *(96 pp., $19.95, Item #21699174, ISBN 1-890490-07-5)*

Fingerstyle Guitar Essentials

Learn fingerstyle techniques, tunings, and arranging from some of the finest teachers around. This practical guide is packed with tips on fingerstyle accompaniment, arranging for solo guitar, single-note licks and double-stops, and playing 12-bar blues. *(96 pp., $19.95, Item #21699145, ISBN 1-890490-06-7)*

Swing Guitar Essentials

An introduction to diverse swing styles, pioneering players, and must-hear recordings. Learn movable jazz chords you can apply to hundreds of songs, swinging soloing techniques, jazz melody basics to use in your own arrangements, and lots more. *(80 pp., $19.95, Item #21699193, ISBN 1-890490-18-0)*

Roots and Blues Fingerstyle Guitar

A treasure trove of traditional American guitar styles by Steve James, one of today's leading roots-music performers, recording artists, and teachers. You'll be inspired and motivated by his clear, accessible arrangements and stories of such masters as Furry Lewis, Sam McGee, and Mance Lipscomb. *(96 pp., $19.95, Item #21699214, ISBN 1-890490-14-8)*

Acoustic Blues Guitar Essentials

Expand your repertoire with this engaging collection of ten great lessons on blues lead, fingerpicking, and slide techniques. Includes six full songs to play. *(80 pp., $19.95, Item #21699186, ISBN 1-890490-10-5)*

Fingerstyle Guitar Masterpieces

12 instrumental compositions and arrangements by today's best fingerstyle players. Hear all the original artist performances on the CD, and then use the clear, accurate transcriptions to bring their songs to life on your guitar. *(66 pp., $16.95, Item #21699222, ISBN 1-890490-13-X)*

For more information on books from String Letter Publishing, or to place an order, please call Music Dispatch at (800) 637-2852 , fax (414) 774-3259, or mail to Music Dispatch, PO Box 13920, Milwaukee, WI 53213. Visit String Letter Publishing on-line at www.stringletter.com.

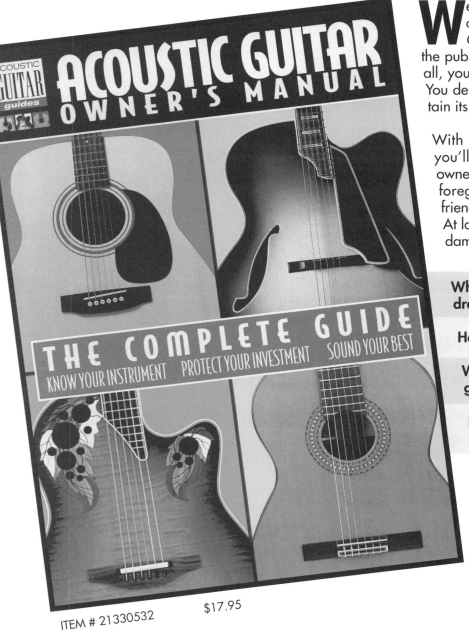